The Influence of the British on Early Southern California

The Sun Never Sets

by Eva Shaw, Ph.D.

Contributions of the English,
Irish, Scottish, Welsh
and Canadians

Dickens Press
Irvine, California

Copyright 2001 by Dickens Press
Published by Dickens Press
P.O. Box 4289, Irvine, California 92616
(800) 230-8158 (orders)

Front Cover: Ellen Browning Scripps, Bob Hope, May Sutton Bundy, James Irvine, Sr., and Citrus Pickers.
Back Cover: William Mulholland

Library of Congress Cataloging-in-Publication Data

Shaw, Eva, 1947-
    The sun never sets : the influence of the British on early Southern
California : contributions of the English, Irish, Scottish, Welsh, and
Canadians / Eva Shaw.
        p. cm.
    Includes bibliographical references and index.
    ISBN 1-880741-32-6 (alk. paper)
    1. California, Southern--Civilization. 2. British
Americans--California, Southern--History.   3. Irish
Americans--California, Southern--History.   4. Scottish
Americans--California, Southern--History.   5. Welsh
Americans--California, Southern--History.   6. Canadian
Americans--California, Southern--History.   7. Immigrants--California,
Southern--History. 8. California, Southern--Ethnic relations. 9.
California--History--To 1846.   10.   United   States--Civilization--British
influences.   I. Title.
    F867 .S55 2001
    979.4'900413--dc21

                                        00-012764

Distributed to the trade by Dickens Press
ISBN 1-880741-32-6
10 9 8 7 6 5 4 3 2 1
First Printing 2001
Printed in Canada

Interior and cover design by Michele Lanci-Altomare
Digital Manipulation by Rick Penn-Kraus
Edited by Jacquelyn Landis

ACKNOWLEDGMENTS

WHILE ON THE SURFACE IT MAY SEEM THAT ONE WRITER OFTEN CREATES A BOOK, THE OPPOSITE IS TRUE. A book is never a singular project. An endeavor, especially one such as this, takes many hands, hearts, and minds. A simple thank-you to those mentioned below and others who have stood by the sidelines listening, encouraging, and mentoring this book, cannot clearly express the gratitude I feel as the writer. Nonetheless, simple words must suffice, and thank you to the following:

Dorothy Hertzog, dear, gracious lady and role model for all those who love and recognize
the contributions of the British and Canadians to early Southern California.

Diane Fallon, my publisher and friend,
for encouraging me and being enthusiastic about the book from the very beginning.

Jacquelyn Landis, my editor, writing colleague and dear friend,
for never failing to find ways to polish the words and ideas I produced.

Michele Lanci-Altomare, graphic designer and gifted book designer,
for creating the visual masterpiece you're now holding.

Linda Heichman and Helene Demeestere, photo researchers,
for spending hours diving through piles of old photos to discover those that are just right.

Karen McKenzie, indexer,
for time well spent to make this book so usable and a valuable tool for the future.

James C. Fallon, researcher,
for the census information that helped substantiate the book.

Richard Hanks, M.A., Project Manager,
Riverside Local History Resource Center, Riverside, California,
for sharing his knowledge and time.

Scott Field, AIA,
for supplying information about Southern California's
famous British-born architect James Parkinson.

Joe Shaw, my husband and lifetime best friend,
for listening to the countless stories. His Celtic ancestors helped settle our country
just as those immigrants you'll read about in these pages.
A huge thank-you for helping me to see the bigger picture,
even while I was bolted down to the minute details,
and for settling the thorny question of "Shall I really include this?"

To all who helped, listened,
added their two cents and brought me back to reality
during the length of this project, thank you.

CONTENTS

Foreword • vii
Introduction • ix
Map • xii

FOREWORD

DURING MY LONG CAREER AS A HISTORY TEACHER IN LOS ANGELES PUBLIC SCHOOLS, I OFTEN
reflected on the irony of being limited to teaching just California history, American history or European history.
After all, my own family history is deeply steeped in its English heritage. Both of my parents came to the United
States from England with their parents before the turn of the twentieth century. What may surprise many is that
they joined an already-thriving English colony right here in Southern California.

My paternal grandfather, William Allen, arrived first, in 1879. Like others before and after him, he came to
Southern California for his health, fleeing the cold, damp English weather for a more temperate climate. He pur-
chased a 500-acre ranch in Pasadena, and he and his family settled in to enjoy a wide circle of English friends.
Anyone familiar with the Pasadena/Altadena/San Marino area is sure to know Allen Avenue, which extends from
Mt. Wilson to the Huntington Library. The street was named for William Allen and serves as the western bound-
ary of Pasadena.

My maternal grandfather, Captain Adolphus G. Sutton of the Royal Navy, arrived with his family in 1893,
also in search of a climate more suitable for his health. He and my grandmother were parents to "The Sutton
Girls," four talented tennis stars. My Aunt May Sutton was the first American winner at Wimbledon in 1905 and
1907, and two other aunts taught tennis at UCLA for many years. My mother, Adele Sutton, was the unknown
Sutton sister.

My mother and my father met in Pasadena, and our family lived in various places around the Los Angeles
area, including Charter Oak and San Marino. I studied history at UCLA, where I met my husband, Walter, and I
completed my Master's degree in California History at Berkeley—not until 1942, however. I had been in Berkeley the preceding summer, working in the Bancroft Library, and decided that was an opportune time to continue
my education. All my life I have been fascinated by the English and Canadian settlement in Southern California.
My first book as a child was a collection of English history stories, and I have traveled to England a number of
times. English history is truly in my blood.

I was first inspired to create a book on the British and Canadian influence on the growth and development
in Southern California by, of all things, a trip to Texas. I was in San Antonio at Christmastime, and while out shopping one day I found an odd book. It was a history of the German pioneers and their settlement in the

Fredericksburg area. I realized that just as I had no idea that German expatriates had so significantly influenced part of Texas, perhaps there existed an equal lack of knowledge about the many influential British and Canadian men and women who had left their mark on Southern California.

Thus this project was born. As you read these pages, I hope the familiar names will delight and surprise you. I further hope you will gain an appreciation for the accomplishments and achievements made by the many British and Canadian citizens who have called Southern California home.

Dorothy Hertzog

INTRODUCTION

IRVINE, DOWNEY, CHAPLIN, SCRIPPS, BULLOCK, CHAFFEE, MULHOLLAND, PICKFORD, SUTTON, GAGE, AND PARKINSON.

The names have connections that run deeper than signs on streets, cities, libraries, movie credits, stores, and public works. These extraordinary men and women, who were born in the British Isles or Canada, influenced early Southern California, and they are the heart of this book.

If the names are already familiar, that should not be a surprise. You may have read about them in history books and heard their names in dedication ceremonies. You may even be familiar with some of the stories behind the headlines. However, there's much more. And even if you were born and raised in Southern California, you may not know the depth of their influence.

People from the British Isles and Canada have engraved Southern California with their determination, energy, ability, and creativity. They have left their mark on this region, as has no other group. Yet, they're often forgotten in the great scheme of things; often their contributions are glossed over and attributed to the work of "immigrants."

Throughout the book you'll read the far-too-brief life stories of those who spent time, love, and money in Southern California. Complete books have been written about these people. Many more could and should be written about each of the influential men and women, yet many have been forgotten over time.

The "Historically Speaking" sections, sprinkled throughout the book, are taken straight from their own words and their diaries and journals. They offer glimpses into heroism and courage, often against odds unimaginable today.

You'll find more information in "City Sketches." The sketches give you insight about how some of the notable communities in Southern California were "born" and their uniqueness in our history. "Portraits" will tell you the stories of individuals who helped shape Southern California.

All these details, like a fine Persian carpet, are woven together to produce the fabric that was the influence from the British Isles and Canada in Southern California. Their legacy is our heritage; their own contributions or their heirs are such a part of our everyday life that we can hardly imagine a time without them. As your mind connects the people, places, and events, the "big picture" will appear about lives and times of those who settled the country from Santa Barbara south to the Mexican border, and from the Pacific Ocean to the Nevada and Arizona state lines.

The events, along with the stories of women and men selected and shared, are included because they were influential. There is no doubt that many thousands have also contributed: good people, honest people, who should be admired. Alas, this book has its limitations, and this account is a broad-brush stroke of one small segment of history. "If all the stories were told," quipped one historian as this book was discussed prior to publication, "you couldn't lift it off the coffee table." It is true. If I could have included every person, place, and event that marked Southern California and pertained to the British flag, the book would have been gargantuan. As it is, I was forced to make decisions, tough ones, on the who, what, when, where, and why of my topic. I hope you approve of the choices. I know they do not adequately cover it, but again, this is a beginning.

One of my goals was to have the book you're holding whet your interest and then allow you to learn more. I hope you'll use the bibliography and histories as jumping-off points for further investigation. That's why you'll find a list of historical societies and important organizations at the end of the book.

In all cases, I have attempted to use documented and reliable sources, yet we must realize that even published material on historical events can be erroneous. Further, historical views change. What was considered important or even disgraceful just twenty years ago may raise nary an eyebrow today.

Historical accounts are an organized collection of people and incidents that, during the process, may or may not be embellished in the system that's used by those who put pen to paper (or today, fingers to a computer's keyboard). It is my hope that, throughout this book, there is as little embellishment as possible; however, without a doubt, there is some. No two accounts or people, for that matter, are alike. Even the personal journals and diaries accessed for this book, in some places contained conflicting information. Does history always reveal truth? Impossible to say, but it's safe to admit that it is revealing.

Here's an example. During the beginning of my research on the British Isles and Canadian influence in Southern California, I discovered a glowing biography, published in 1930, of a British film star who called Hollywood home. The source stated Mr. X "is adored throughout the world," and he "is probably one of the best-known men in America." Since I had never heard of Mr. X, I dug further. The results were intriguing and I was startled. This investigation proved how quickly things change. I learned that America's "favorite" film star died shortly after publication of that book, amidst drug dealings, gambling, and assorted scandals one might read about today on the cover of a supermarket tabloid.

For ease in reading you'll find references to "British Isles" and/or "Canada" throughout the book. These references include those who were born in or those who have easily traceable ancestors from the British Isles, including England, Ireland, Scotland, Wales, and from Canada, which, of course, was under the British flag. The decision on what terms to use was exhausting and caused a number of enthusiastic arguments. Some suggested that "this is right," and then another countered that it would, in fact, be gravely insulting. Terms can never fit every ethnic group; I apologize to those from Ireland, England, Scotland, and Wales who might be offended by the final selection. Please know that no offense was intended.

As you read the stories, the tales of heroism and folly, of inventive industrialism and sheer determination, keep in mind that these, too, are your predecessors. So the next time you're driving through Riverside, you'll be able to remark that Riverside was the home of an English Colony and supposedly one of the first places in California where polo matches were held. Santa Monica holds the same honor. When you board the train at Los Angeles Union Station, drive past Los Angeles City Hall (of *Dragnet* fame), or visit the original campus of the University of Southern California, you can tell friends that these remarkable structures were the work of British architect John Parkinson. And when you turn on the tap and fill a glass of water, you can thank Irishman William Mulholland for helping to bring water to a very thirsty area.

Please read the book straight through or sit and enjoy the sidebars. Marvel at the old photos. Pick out the quotes, quips, and sketches of historical Southern California. It's my hope that you'll be amazed, delighted, and inspired, as I have been, by the British Isles/Canadian influence in early Southern California.

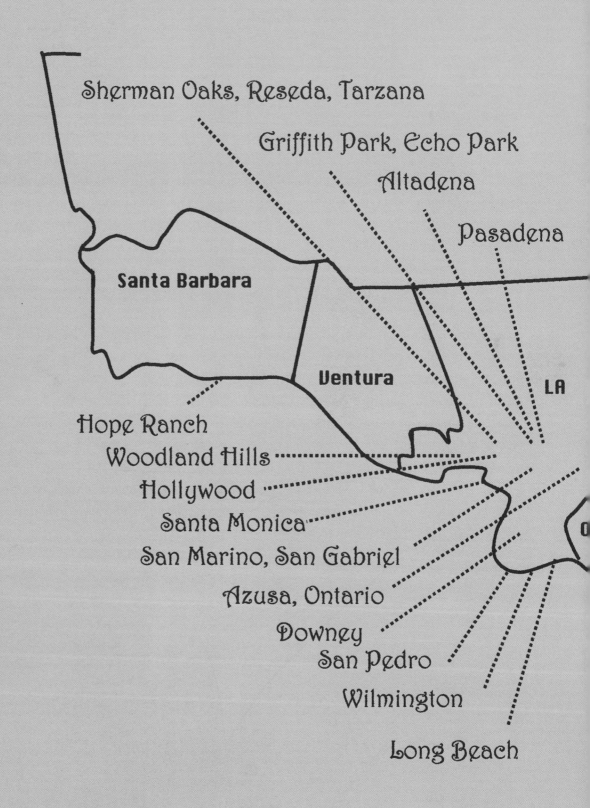

Sherman Oaks, Reseda, Tarzana

Griffith Park, Echo Park

Altadena

Pasadena

Santa Barbara

Ventura

LA

Hope Ranch

Woodland Hills

Hollywood

Santa Monica

San Marino, San Gabriel

Azusa, Ontario

Downey

San Pedro

Wilmington

Long Beach

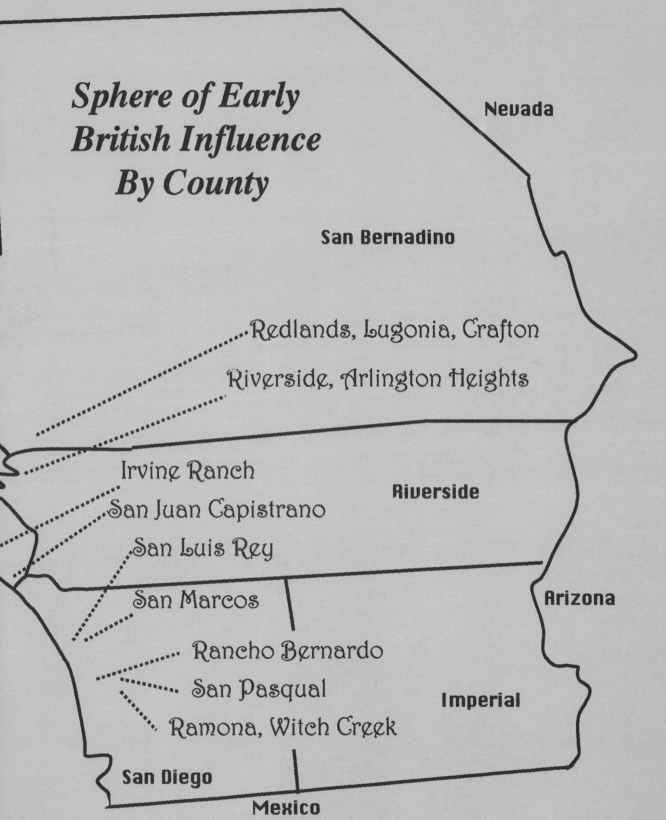

Sphere of Early British Influence By County

Nevada

San Bernadino

Redlands, Lugonia, Crafton

Riverside, Arlington Heights

Irvine Ranch

San Juan Capistrano

San Luis Rey

Riverside

Arizona

San Marcos

Rancho Bernardo

San Pasqual

Imperial

Ramona, Witch Creek

San Diego

Mexico

CHAPTER 1

New Albion Sets the Stage for British Isles and Canadian Influence

Are you aware that if Queen Elizabeth I had had her way, we might be calling the hood of our cars the bonnet? Or that we might spell "color," "colour," and speak with a British accent?

According to historical accounts, the first individual from the British Isles to step on California soil was none other than that swash-buckling buccaneer, English sea captain Sir Francis Drake. Not only did he walk in California, but he claimed the very ground we often walk on for his queen.

It happened on June 17, 1579. The new land was christened New Albion or Nova Albion, in some sources a literary term for Britain. It is understood that Drake and others had plans to colonize the area, although New Albion was never realized. Thus most of us do not have English accents, nor are we the royal subjects of Her Majesty Queen Elizabeth II.

The intrigue in this story reads like an "Unsolved Mystery" one might see on television. Weary from the months-long voyage, Drake and his crew aboard the *Golden Hind* were carrying a huge cargo of Spanish and Dutch plunder and needed to take shelter to repair the ship before heading west and eventually back to England. The place chosen was a small bay and selected because the inhabitants were "friendly." According to accounts, this meant that there were no hostile moves against the Englishmen, who stayed there until July 23. Short trips were made inland, but San Francisco Bay, contrary to the popular urban myth, wasn't discovered at that time. Drake's landing was around that area, either 30 miles north or 30 miles south. There's no evidence to determine the exact landing site; even the Drake Plates don't yield a clue. The reason they never supposedly found the bay was probably due to the traditional San Francisco fog.

The accounts of Drake's trip along the California coast document that the indigenous people may have thought that the visitors were gods or the reincarnated souls of their dead. According to historian Philip S. Rush, author of *A History of the Californias,* "At a ceremonial, Drake was 'crowned' by the head chieftain, and the Englishmen considered this a sign that the natives submitted to English sovereignty, although each could understand only a few words of the other's language."

Supposedly the Native Americans gathered in large groups. It's imagined that the English were a curious lot to their eyes, with strange clothing, skin color, and customs. The English "conquerors" read chapters from the Bible, said prayers, and sang psalms. This is said to have been the first Protestant service in California.

Before leaving California to sail west, Drake supposedly nailed a plate of brass and an English sixpence to a post, as proof of ownership of the land for his queen. The plate is said to have read as follows:

Bee it knowne vnto all men by these presents ivne 17 1579 by the grace of God and in the name of herr maiesty qveen Elizabeth of England and herr svccessors forever I take possession of this kingdome whose kind and people freely resign their right and title in the whole land vnto herr maiesties keeping now named by me to bee known vnto all men as nova albio. Francis Drake.

In 1936, a brass plate was discovered just inland from what we now call Drake's Bay. Many historians believed, at that time, it was the true documentation that Drake had landed. Then again in 1949, 1956, and 1962, other plates were discovered. Even today, most people believe that there are more opinions than can be correct as to which plate, if any, is authentic.

Sir Francis Drake may have been the first Britisher to have stepped on California soil.
Courtesy of the Photo Collection/
Los Angeles Public Library

THE FIRST MYSTERY PLATE

On a balmy afternoon in July 1936, Beryle Shinn went walking in the area around Point San Quentin and San Francisco Bay. Tossing rocks down a hillside, he noticed an object that was nearly covered by a rock. Times were tough, and the story goes that Shinn thought the metal might be useful if he needed to make some repairs on his auto.

But when handling it, he noticed there seemed to be writing on it. Soap and water revealed more, and the novelty was dragged out for friends and neighbors. Some months later, according to a report by the California Historical Society, Shinn showed the plate to Professor Herbert Bolton, from the history department at the University of California, Berkeley. Bolton said, "I have been telling my students for years to keep an eye out for Drake's Plate."

In February of 1937, Bolton declared, "The authenticity of the tablet seems to me beyond all reasonable doubt." Bolton believed that the artifact was the exact plate posted by Drake when he landed in California. The plate matched the description in a book called *The World Encompassed*, by Francis Fletcher, a captain aboard Drake's *Golden Hind*. It's interesting to note that this book was not published until 1628, so it was probably written from secondary information, that of an observer to the event.

Fletcher had written,

Before we went from thence, our generall caused to be set vp, a monument of our being there; as also of her maiesties, and successors right and title to that kingdome, namely a plate of brasse, fast nailed to a great and firme post; whereon is engrauven her graces name, and the day and yeare of our arriuall there, and of the free giuing vp, of the prouince and kingdome, by the kind and the people, into here maiesties hands: together with his highnesse picture, and armes in a piece of sixpence currant English monie, shewing it selfe by a hole made of purpose through the plate; vnderneath was likewise engrauen the name of our generall &c.

However, the plate has gone through numerous testings, including microscope examination, macrophoto documentation, and ultrasonic exams from the Lawrence Livermore Laboratory and Oxford (England) University, among others. A statement by R. E. M. Hedges, Research Laboratory for Archaeology and the History of Art at Oxford University, sums up other opinions: "I do not think they [the results of the analysis] can provide unequivocal proof of the authenticity or of the forgery of the plate."

Whether the plate was really posted by Drake or simply is a huge hoax still remains a mystery, although the most recent scientific review indicates that the plates are rolled brass, which was not available in Drake's time.

British Interest in Early California

Spanish influence in early California is often the only authority recognized, and thousands of history books expound on the work of Spain's missionaries. Many of those same books, though, talk about America in the 1840s and how "Manifest Destiny" was being shouted as a claim to the United States' right to rule from the Atlantic to the Pacific.

This claim was to be realized by force if necessary. The United States government was ready to take Texas, which had recently won independence from Mexico, and California seemed to be the logical next step. However, England was also eyeing that portion of North America lying along the Pacific Ocean, and the leadership of the United States knew it, taking measures to prepare to defend its own land. Keep in mind that Mexico also assumed ownership of Lower California.

Nonetheless, the U.S. Pacific Squadron, under the command of Commodore Catesby and Captain Roger AP Jones, had five vessels with 116 guns. The English Pacific squadron had four superior ships and 104 guns.

Jones headed north, nervously waiting to be attacked by the British fleet. But in September Jones received a message warning that the United States was about to declare war on Mexico. On October 19, 1842, Jones entered Monterey harbor, again expecting to battle with the British fleet, but as accounts reveal, accepted the state of California for the United States without any battles.

So, if the British were that interested, where were they? To find out, we have to look back even before Manifest Destiny.

The British had been seduced by rumors of a Northwest Passage since the eighteenth century, and they still had hopes of finding it. Britisher Alexander Forbes, a merchant in Tepic, Mexico, wrote about California in his 1839 book, *A History of Upper and Lower California,* and talked about the possibility of British investors taking California in recompense for a $50 million debt owed to them by Mexico.

British newspapers picked up the story and promoted the plan. British minister to Mexico, Richard Pakenham, also keen on the project, recommended that London accept the offer. In California there was favorable sentiment for a British takeover. While it may have been wishful thinking or media hype, a delegation of Californians called on the British consul at Monterey, James Forbes, to say that the area should become a British protectorate.

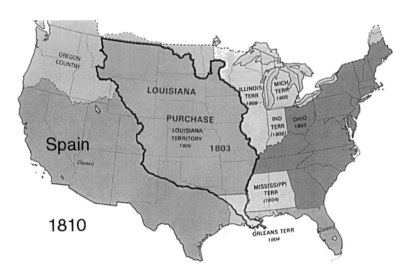

1810

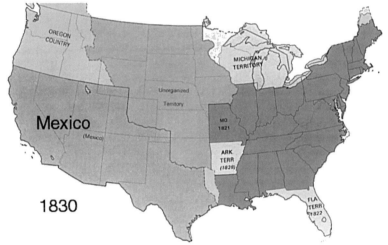

1830

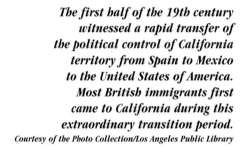

The first half of the 19th century witnessed a rapid transfer of the political control of California territory from Spain to Mexico to the United States of America. Most British immigrants first came to California during this extraordinary transition period.

Courtesy of the Photo Collection/Los Angeles Public Library

1850
California Statehood

While little resulted from this recommendation, rumors continued to bubble, often promoted by American expansionists who were anxious to have the United States take over California and stop the British invasion.

According to historical records, a young Irish priest, Eugene McNamara, may have come up with an enthusiastic scheme to take over the entire area of lower and upper California.

As the story goes, with the blessings of British officials, Father McNamara traveled to Santa Barbara on the British warship Juno, in 1846, where he asked California's Mexican Governor Pio Pico for a land grant to settle Irish farmers. One must remember that all of Ireland was deep in poverty; the Great Potato Famine was still devastating the nation. Irish families were starving from the scarcity of food. The economic conditions were desperate.

Father McNamara may have had the gift of Blarney or perhaps his heartfelt plea was sincere. He talked of settling a colony of 10,000 Irish in California on a site of 3,000 square leagues. A league was a typical measurement of land; a square league comprises approximately 4,430 acres.

The Mexican provincial assembly met in Los Angeles and approved the priest's request. Later, so the story goes, Pico backdated the order so that it was signed before the American occupation of California. Nothing came of the scheme to have Irish Catholics settle in California as a means to further British presence in the new land. Why the scheme did not materialize is unclear; however, it is an intriguing side note to history.

YANG-NA
Los Angeles

On August 1, 1769, Gaspar de Portola headed a Spanish expedition north to what is now Los Angeles, but called Yang-na by the Native American tribes. De Portola called the area El Rio de Nuestra Señora la Reina de los Angeles de Porciuncula, or The River of Our Lady the Queen of the Angels of Porciuncula. The Franciscans, however, preferred a San Gabriel site for their mission. Was Los Angeles too barren? Perhaps.

In 1781, 44 Mexican colonists established rustic dwellings in the area. The first Americans arrived using the roadstead port (a place where the road ended at the shore and cargo was loaded from boats to wagons) of San Pedro, and beginning in 1805, U.S. vessels began docking out from the harbor. Los Angeles was little affected by the revolution that changed Mexico from Spanish rule to an independent nation. The city's isolation (as an undesirable outpost) allowed farmers and ranchers to run the area as they saw fit. In 1840, the first party of American pioneers settled in the area, led by William Workman and John Rowland.

After the Treaty of Guadalupe Hidalgo, which ceded California from Mexico to the United States, the settlement grew. At one time it was called the "Queen of the Cow Counties" because of its role supplying beef, citrus, and foodstuffs for the gold miners and their families. During the 1850s and 1860s, Los Angeles had a reputation for violence; the crime rate was reportedly acknowledged at one murder per day.

In 1876, seven years after Collis P. Huntington's Big Four (consisting of Leland Stanford, Huntington, Mark Hopkins, and Charles Crocker) established the transcontinental railroad, Los Angeles was connected to the rest of the country. After a land boom and bust were only a memory, oil was discovered in the Signal Hill area of the city. Edward L. Doheny, of Irish descent, and Charles A. Canfield drilled the first well in a residential front lawn in Signal Hill in 1892, and soon there were as many as 1500 wells around the city. Once again, Los Angeles and surrounding communities were on the up side of the boom. It seemed nothing could stop Los Angeles now.

1909 Los Angeles, long before it became a cosmopolitan city.
Courtesy of the Photo Collection/Los Angeles Public Library

Water was a constant concern, however. The Los Angeles River had sustained residents, but now that the city was established and crime somewhat contained, immigration again was soaring. Water was sure to run out. Headlines of the *Los Angeles Times* talked about "water starvation." How could this be happening?

William Mulholland, a self-educated engineer and Irish immigrant, was chief engineer of the Los Angeles Department of Water and Power. He proposed the unheard of: The City should develop a system to bring in water from the Owens River Valley, some 200 miles north of the city. While the scheme was daring and daunting, it seemed the only solution. Crews began in 1908 to dig aqueducts, tunnels, siphons, and dams. Los Angeles would not die of thirst. In 1913 when the floodgates opened, Mulholland was there to take the glory and supposedly turned to the delegation and said, "There it is, gentlemen. Take it."

In the early years of the twentieth century, Los Angeles leaders improved the harbor in time to profit from the increased shipping trade now possible by the completion of the Panama Canal. Additionally, Los Angeles and Hollywood were becoming synonymous with movies and movie stars.

And the city continues to move forward, now into the twenty-first century.

Gold Rushes in and Progress Comes to the State

When gold was discovered at Sutter's Mill in January 1848, Northern California became the focal point of the rush for riches. Most headed straight for the gold fields east of San Francisco; about 50,000 arrived in 1849. Most were industrious, good-hearted workers. Their dream? To gather up the quick wealth that was told in story, song, and newspaper, and return to the comforts of the East. Some were former gold seekers from the British Isles and Australia who had heard the news thousands of miles away that gold was filtering through the streams, lying there to be snatched up by the handful.

Towns sprang up along the rivers, most merely tents or shanties. Some small cities put down roots and they were so deep you can still find them today. San Francisco, an outfitting point for the gold fields, bulged to over 5,000 in population in 1849, and this was merely the beginning of gold fever.

The cities and towns, the settlements and the vast frontier of Southern California, were not greatly affected by the gold rush. But the cattle ranchers of the time were having their own gold rush: supplying beef to the hungry miners and those who would settle.

In April 1848, Congress established a regular mounted mail route from San Diego to San Francisco that ran through the San Fernando Valley and north using the trails of the San Joaquin routes. On August 14 of that same year, Postmaster General C. Johnson authorized opening of post offices in all the major cities along the coast: San Diego, San Pedro, Santa Barbara, San Luis Obispo, and Monterey. Postage was 40 cents for a half-ounce. In today's currency that could equate to about $5 for a regular letter.

It was time for California to become a state many believed, except, of course, the Mexican government who firmly had rights in Southern California. With the signing of the Treaty of Guadalupe Hidalgo by representatives of the American and Mexican governments on February 2, 1848, it seemed all was heading toward statehood for California.

FROM *CALIFORNIA THE WONDERFUL,*
by Historian and Poet Edwin Markham

Writing about Los Angeles before the discovery at Sutter's Mill…

"You meet native Californians, wide-hatted Mexicans, now and then a Spaniard of the old blue stock, a sprinkle of Indians and the trousered man in his shirt and cue. You see the old broad-brimmed, thick-walled adobes that betray the early days. You hear somebody swearing in Spanish, grumbling German, vociferating Italian, parleying in French, rattling China and talking English.

"You read Spanish, French, German and English newspapers, all printed in Los Angeles. It is as many-tongued as a Mediterranean sea-port, and hospitable as a grandee.

"Yesterday and to-day are strangely blended. You stroll among thousands of vines that are ninety years old and yet in full bearing. You pass a garden just rendered from the dust and ashes of the wilderness. You pluck an orange from a tree that was venerable when Charles the Fourth was king of Spain, and you meet a man who has sat down to wait six years for his first fruit.

"A drive through the old quarter of the city takes you to the heart of Mexico, with the low-eaved fronts, the windows sunk like niches in the walls, the Italic-faced old porticoes, the lazy dogs dozing about in the sun. In ten minutes you are whirled between two long lines of new-made Edens whence Eve was never driven; such wealth of color, such clouds of fragrance, such luxuriance of vegetation."

The news reached California in August that President Polk had agreed to the treaty, and meetings for statehood were implemented. The first Constitutional Convention of California met in Colton Hall, Monterey. It was said that it was the only building in the state that was large enough to hold the gathering.

From The *National Geographic Magazine,* "Southern California at Work," November 1934, Frederick Simpich writes…

"About Los Angeles, there is something unblurred and youthful—a certain exuberance and eagerness to be occupied that shows through its pleasure-resort makeup.

"The gold rush of '49 passed it by. It was still a village when Lincoln freed the slaves, and as late as the 1870's many of its official documents were written in Spanish. It had a bad name in early days; people called it the world's wickedness place. One mayor resigned, temporarily, to help with a public lynching! In one night a mob hanged 18 Chinese, and preachers closed their churches in despair."

Portrait

JOSEPH SNOOK
The Love Story of an English Mariner, California Don

Joseph Snook was born in 1798 in the Dorsetshire town of Weymouth, on the southern coast of England. Snook came from a long family history of farmers and would have probably remained in that profession except that at an early age he was apprenticed to the captain of a merchant ship. At that time, many shipping lines trained their own officers, and according to historian Ruth Collings (*The Journal of San Diego History,* Fall 1997), Snook probably learned to read and write and gained his seamanship and navigation skills during the apprenticeship program.

Why or how Snook came to California was most assuredly due to his work. On his first trip, he was master of the *Ayacucho,* a 232-ton brig belonging to Stephen Anderson of the

James Goldie Company, a Scottish commercial house with a British connection, leaving La Libertat, Peru, and arriving in Monterey 42 days later.

Snook must have been enchanted with what he saw, since he continued to visit from 1832 to 1839 when he was the captain of a German merchant ship, the brig *Catalina*. The ship brought manufactured items to California ports, delivered dispatches, letters, newspapers, carried local produce up and down the territory, conveyed passengers, and transported huge quantities of hides and tallow.

Snook decided that his future lay in California. Collings writes, "In making this decision he was thinking not only of himself but also of his impoverished family back in England. Here in California, there was land for the asking, tillable land to provide the prosperity for his brothers that would have been impossible in Weymouth."

In order to have the power to "ask" for land, however, Snook had to become a Catholic and a Mexican citizen. On April 29, 1833, he petitioned for naturalization (the letter was destroyed in the San Francisco earthquake and fire) and was baptized Francisco de Sales on November 3, 1835. San Francisco was Snook's first choice of residency on an 8,877-acre rancho north of the city. He called it Rancho de Tomales. He hired laborers to build a 12-by-15-foot cabin of logs "as thick as a man's thigh and plastered over with clay." He stocked the ranch with livestock and began a life as a don.

The decision to settle in California, it is imagined, was also an affair of the heart. Snook had fallen in love with a lovely young San Diego woman, Maria Antonia Alvarado. History remains vague on the courtship between Snook and Alvarado, and the next account is that of December 2, 1837, when they married in San Diego's presidio chapel. The couple traveled north to the rancho, but apparently Maria Antonia did not take well to the misty, cooler climate, which was much like Snook's native English coast. Sometime later, husband and wife returned to Southern California and made a home there.

Snook continued as a sea captain, often away for months, but when he was home he settled in what are now the Rancho Bernardo and San Marcos regions of San Diego County. A wealthy landowner, he was much the English squire of the time. The don's future was clouded by war, however, and while Captain Snook was sailing north, it is supposed that his ship may have been delivering ammunition to the anti-American, pro-Spanish-Mexican troops.

Joseph Snook was a sea captain who became a trader and landowner in San Diego.
Courtesy of the San Diego Historical Society

Meanwhile, Californians and Americans battled at San Pasqual and Rancho San Bernardo.

As the fierce battles continued, Maria Antonia lost her brother and father before the Treaty of Guadalupe Hidalgo was signed.

Historical documents are unclear, yet somehow Snook was involved in the fight to keep California under Mexican control. The only references to Snook's death are the words of Robert Clift to colleague Henry Fitch. Clift wrote, "I was astonished to hear of the sudden death of Captain Snook. It must from accounts have been a distressing affair."

By the time the war between Mexico and the United States ended with the Treaty of Guadalupe Hidalgo on February 2, 1848, Joseph Snook's dream of building an estate for his English family was over. Records show that although Snook left the real estate in San Diego to his English relatives, and they attempted to sue for the possessions, his wife exercised her right to the property. She remarried and lived on the property.

Although little is known about this early English don, he may have been one of the first people from the British Isles to establish roots in Southern California.

This overview of California history must include the heated debate on the issue of slavery and state's rights that were festering in Washington and throughout the Union. The California Convention voted unanimously to make California a free state. The constitution, it is said, was patterned after the constitutions of Iowa and New York.

A Mexican law, very cutting edge at the time, recognized that women could retain title to real estate owned before marriage and share equally in community property, and this was incorporated into the new constitution. Another stipulation was added: Duelists would be disfranchised.

The first California legislature convened in San Jose on December 15, 1849; it was a non-partisan gathering of 16 senators and 36 members of the assembly. The first president pro tem of the Senate was E. Kirby Chamberlin of San Diego. But just because California had voted to be free didn't mean that all was settled on the issues that were ripping apart the Union at the time.

On February 23, 1850, President Zachary Taylor asked Congress to admit California to the Union. Southern senators hotly protested. Their cry was, "California's new anti-slavery constitution violated the Missouri Compromise." Henry Clay was at the forefront of a bitter fight to have the state admitted, and finally on September 9, 1850, Millard Fillmore (who became president when Taylor died) signed the bill that admitted California into the Union.

When California joined the Union in 1850, the southern portion of the state had everything against it, if one were making odds on the future success of a location. All eyes were turned to San Francisco and its resources, including untapped gold fields.

Southern California was scantily populated, desert-like for the most part with great rolling agricultural areas, right only for cattle and sheep. If you've ever driven on Highway 10 from Los Angeles, past Banning and Beaumont toward Palm Springs, you have an idea of the texture of much of Southern California before freeways and people invaded.

Settlements dotted the countryside, but the dots were hard to connect. Robert M. Fogelson writes about the beginnings of the community of Los Angeles in *The Fragmented Metropolis: Los Angeles, 1850-1930:* "It was simply a nondescript agricultural village with 1,610 people, no railroads, and few streets or other public improvements. It was isolated, geographically and economically, from the large population centers of the United States and Europe." There were plenty of minuses against Southern California ever rivaling the northern part of the state or anywhere else in the Union. The area had no natural harbor or obvious resources like timber and gold; there were no large bodies of fresh water or fast-moving rivers that could ensure commerce or power for factories.

Yet with these points against it, all of Southern California still sprang up like a much-hoped-for and unexpected artesian well, turning Mexican villages into proud, cultured towns and cities. The area mushroomed like no other in history, and Southern California went from sage-brush stopover to metropolitan area in less than 80 years, to become one of the most powerful and populated areas on the Pacific Coast.

People from the British Isles and Canada were there. They produced the culture and the spirit that today is Southern California.

Portrait

A BRITISH RANCHERO IN OLD CALIFORNIA

Henry Dalton stepped from a ship as a British citizen and within less than ten years became a prominent merchant and guiding force in early Southern California.

Biographer Sheldon Jackson writes, "In the course of his long life spanning nearly eighty-one years, he fled from the tedious routine of a London apprenticeship to the equally brief encounter as an eager store clerk in South America." Dalton, however, was not destined to remain a clerk or, for that matter, to work for others.

His future was in Southern California and as a gentleman of a great rancho in what is now Azusa. Although Dalton prided himself as a man who didn't meddle, he became politically active and closely followed the expanding British presence throughout the world. Perhaps he hoped that England would take on the Mexican government and occupy California; many from the British Isles had similar hopes. Dalton is said to have reveled in the exploits of the British navy and conquests, including Waterloo.

Jackson writes, "During his four decades in Southern California, Dalton experienced difficulties typical of many rancheros. A fraudulent survey which not only took his lands but was upheld by the courts, squatters who took his choice lands and his water, and a political system that failed to protect his property rights, left him understandably embittered and explain why he remained a British citizen to the end."

But life, even with the challenges enumerated by Jackson, was mixed with pleasures for Dalton. Marrying and raising a healthy, happy family, he created Rancho Azusa and it became a mecca for hospitality. While you may not find him listed amongst those who were instrumental in the transformation of California into the State of California, he was as prominent as Reid and Stearns and Sutter. Further, Dalton's efforts contributed to culture, education, and new farming methods that would forever change our state.

Henry Dalton was a prominent landowner who established Rancho Azusa.
Courtesy of the USC Regional Historical Collection

A NOTE:
The Dalton Collection, more than 2,500 pieces of correspondence, business papers and bound volumes documenting Dalton's life and work are in the Huntington Library.

Railway Opens More of Southern California

California suffered less during the reconstruction period of the Civil War than other states in the Union, but California sorely needed transportation and communication if it was to grow. In 1853 Congress had allotted $150,000 for surveys for a railroad from the Missouri River to the Pacific Coast, but no recommendations had been adopted to implement it.

In June 1861, the Southern Pacific Railroad Company was organized with Leland Stanford, president; Collis P. Huntington, vice-president; Mark Hopkins, treasurer; and Charles Crocker, secretary. They came to be known as California's "Big Four."

On July 1, 1862, President Lincoln signed an act passed by Congress to provide construction of a railroad and telegraph line from the Missouri River to the Pacific Coast. The Southern Pacific would build the California end of the transcontinental railroad while the Union Pacific would build westward.

With the completion of the railroad in 1869, the grain-growing industry of California had a resurgence that would continue in strength until the land bust of the late 1880s.

Portrait

HUGO REID
The Mysterious Scot

ℋugo Reid, originally from the County of Renfrew, Scotland, brought British Isles' style of living to early Southern California. Reid, educated at Cambridge University, is rarely mentioned these days, even in history books. He lived the leisurely life of a gentleman rancher where the Huntington Library now stands in San Marino. Reid was not alone in his gentleman rancher persona, as another Britisher, John Forster, from Liverpool, England, was a landholder in Rancho Santa Margarita, north of San Diego in what is now the San Juan Capistrano area.

Reid's biographer, Susanna Bryant Dankin, writes that he enjoyed being a "literary dilettante far more than a competitive business[man]. As a result, he never made a fortune to compare with Stearns' land empire." Yet, his contribution to history is immeasurable.

His letters and diaries provide a clear vision of what life was in the booming rancho days of early Southern California. Some records are still available for the serious researcher in the Huntington Library; Reid's essays are in the Bancroft Library at the University of California, Berkeley.

Reid, like the fictional heroes in stories by Helen Hunt Jackson, including *Ramona*, married a native Californian. To see the big picture, it's intriguing to note that Helen Hunt Jackson's work, much like her colleague and friend Harriet Beecher Stowe, brought public attention to the long-suffering plight of Native Americans. Although for many it's sheer speculation, Reid's own romance is considered the basis for Ramona. As an historical side note, the producer and director of the world-famous *Ramona* Pageant, which inspired scores of other historical dramatic productions, was created by Garnet Holme, originally from Canada. Of further note, Hunt's work also began the Mission Revival movement in architecture, which spawned other noteworthy and innovative schools of design.

Doña Victoria, Reid's Native American wife, was reportedly a great beauty. Writer William Heath Davis, author of the classic *Seventy-five Years in California,* once paid a two-month visit to the ranch and describes that "they were most prosperous." Davis says, "They

THE HUGO REID FAMILY

offered gay and unstinting hospitality from their beautiful Rancho de Santa Anita to whoever came that way."

Hugo Reid, a contemporary and friend of Henry Dalton, was a true pioneer. He was a member of the first constitutional convention, although the convention met without authority of the United States government. Dankin writes about the convention: "Forty-eight men of varied nationality, age, religion, occupation and political conviction were crowded into the modest adobe called Colton Hall, 'disputed like the devil at home' to quote Reid." Arguments circled on women's rights and the rights for minorities. "But they accomplished their purpose in six weeks of hard work."

Always a solitary, thoughtful man, for several months in 1851 Reid disappeared, simply walking away from his family and comfortable surroundings. He had long planned a series of Indian essays, and that's exactly what the scholar was doing. In May he reappeared, tired, malnourished, but satisfied; the essays were complete.

William Rand, editor of the new *Los Angeles Star* accepted them gratefully and with real interest. He hired Reid as the San Gabriel correspondent and in February, the editor announced that the newspaper would run a series of articles "upon the manners, customs, et cetera, of the Indians, from the pen of Hugo Reid, Esq., a gentleman well conversant with the subject with which he treats."

The essays began with a description of the language, then moved to customs, religion and legends of local tribes. He wrote about the Spaniards' arrival and their cruel treatment of the Native Americans. He concluded with a poignant account of their dismal living conditions, and with his mighty words brought much local and national interest. On the heels of his success with the essays, Reid compiled a list of vocabulary and complete language manual of Indian and English of the Southern California tribes.

Before finishing this task, Reid, who was never physically strong, fell ill and died on December 12, 1852. The world not only lost a fine Scotsman and gentlemen, but one of the first California writers and historians to take time to chronicle the stories of the Native Californians. Hugo Reid left a legacy of what life was like for those inhabitants of Southern California well before any Spaniard or American stepped on the scene. Even today, one can visit the Hugo Reid Adobe at the Los Angeles Arboretum.

In the settlements that sprang to life during the boom, many were formed by "colonies" composed of people who were determined to make Southern California their home. Quite a few were people of specific religious faiths. For instance, the Indiana Colony, settled in 1873, purchased the old San Pasqual Rancho and developed the city of Pasadena. A colony of Iowa Quakers founded the city of Whittier. The "village" of Riverside, once known as the English Colony or New England Colony, became a city thanks to the land boom of the 1870s and the citrus crops, along with the financial backing of English funding.

Some towns were strictly developed to entice migrants from the East, the British Isles, and Canada. Pasadena is an example and lured many who came to Southern California for their health. There were immigrants from the British Isles in Imperial and Ventura counties, too. Places like Lugonia and Crafton, near Redlands; Witch Creek, Forster, and San Pasqual City and San Luis Rey in San Diego County; Linda Rosa in Riverside County; and Alosta, Palomares, and Marquette, just east of the city of Los Angeles, were but a few.

The Great Land Boom was a land bust by the end of the 1880s. Land prices plummeted, many latecomers suffered financial ruin, and yet thousands stayed on. More came for the climate. As historian Philip S. Rush says, "Southern California as a whole benefited by its thousands of new citizens, who enjoyed its unrivalled climate, one thing not affected by boom and bust."

"The question of health has induced perhaps a larger percentage of immigration than another single cause. As a last resort invalids who have tried the most favored health resorts of the world turn to Southern California as their last earthly hope. Alas! In many cases no climate can do more than to bring temporary relief and prolong the life beyond what could be hoped for in a climate more violent.

"In instances, not a few, where death seemed inevitable, this climate has wrought a cure. As to the absolute certainty of benefit in any given case, no one can say in advance. With abundance of fruit and the chance to be in the sunshine and open air so much of the time, the probabilities are in favor of benefit to almost any case of chronic sickness. However, an actual trial must be made, and where it is practicable this should be done before a permanent removal is made."

—FROM "WHAT A GENTLEMAN OBSERVED IN AN EIGHT MONTHS' RESIDENCE,"
LOS ANGELES DAILY TIMES, APRIL 15, 1882

The rivalry between Los Angeles and San Diego continued, and even today some Angelinos look down upon San Diego as a sleepy second cousin. Those who live in the desert think the coastal cities are impossibly crowded, much like they did during the boom periods.

With population numbers soaring, Southern California was on the map for good. There were more financial peaks and valleys ahead for the area as World War I changed the face of the sleepy suburbs, and the Great Depression brought more workers to a land that was already filled by its residents, all looking for jobs.

ALTADENA

$\mathcal{P}$art of the original Indiana Colony, the area of what is now the lovely community of Altadena was once known as the Highland Slope. In the 1938 book *Altadena*, historian Sarah Nobel Ives writes that the area was dotted with poppy fields and "We began to grow, getting our impetus as the lands were supplied with water and improved." The real boom for the community happened in the 1880s when families, including the Allens who established the Sphinx Ranch in northwest Altadena in 1878, settled the area.

Ives continues, "This is a little community of homes, mutual needs, mutual understandings, mutual aspirations for the good of all. So intimately do our lives touch that, whether we are the candlestick maker or the one who buys candlesticks, we are ready to do or accept a favorite in the true spirit of equality."

While travelers today might see a sprawling community, the feeling of "old, home-like Altadena" remains when one visits the city and the historical landmarks.

Altadena was home to the Sphinx Ranch and to a large colony of British immigrants.
Courtesy of the Pasadena Historical Museum.

27

Farm laborers posing, circa 1880.
Courtesy of the Riverside Museum

CHAPTER **2**

Influence in Agriculture

When tourists and residents think of Southern California, they most often talk of sunshine and oranges. That follows quickly with a dissertation about having access to the best produce on the planet.

It's a long tradition that California and agriculture have been linked since the rancho days when Southern California was still part of Mexico. Farmers of all nationalities filtered into the area. For instance, British citizen Don Juan Forster (in various reference sources referred to as John Forester) came to California and married California Governor Pio Pico's sister. In 1845, the governor deeded his brother-in-law the rancho, called amongst other names Santa Margarita Ranch, near San Diego. In 1875, Forster bought the Mission San Juan Capistrano for $750. Forster later sold the land and property to Richard Egan, a superior court judge originally from Ireland and instrumental in defining the boundaries between Orange and Los

Angeles counties. Egan built a fine house on the land, and he and his family were active in the British social circle of the times. Today, part of Forster's holdings are in the hands of the Girl Scouts of America, and called El Potrero de la Cienega, a campground of 390 acres in San Diego's Cleveland National Forest.

Cattle and sheep grazed for miles of open territory that is now inhabited by red-roofed stuccos dotting suburbia.

The transition between Mexican-held land and the ownership by immigrants from the United States and the British Empire came in stages. Though frequently called "Spanish ranchos," most of the huge land holdings were granted by the Mexican government after 1836. The title applicants (rancheros) sought locations that had accessibility to water and cheap workers, particularly Native American laborers.

More than fifty land grants were issued in Southern California during this period, 1820 to 1835. In the American period, title holders were expected to establish their rights under the U.S. Land Law of 1851, which proved difficult for many original landowners. The majority of Mexican rancheros lost title owing to tax debts and fatal droughts.

Irishman Nicholas Den, Scotsman Hugo Reid, Britisher Don Juan Forster, Abel Stearns, Benjamin Davis Wilson, Juan Warner, William Wolfskill, and others, came to California before statehood and were amongst those who had received original Spanish grants, yet were able to produce legal deeds to their land. The drought period, according to historians including Kevin Starr, contributed to the ranchos being turned into Anglo-style subdivided ranches, and by the 1880s, many ranchos, especially in Los Angeles county were subdivided and sprang into towns and cities. It was at this time that James Irvine and his business partners began buying up the ranches from such owners as Reid and Wolfskill.

Rancho San Pedro and Rancho Los Palos Verdes became the ports of Wilmington and San Pedro. Rancho Los Alamitos and Rancho Los Cerritos became Long Beach.

While cattle and sheep "owned" the years before 1870, as the land was subdivided into smaller ranches and farms, one crop can be pointed to as having the greatest impact on Southern California. It's citrus. The seeds of the citrus industry were actually planted long before the gold rush. As untold thousands flocked into the hills and invaded Northern California, scurvy debilitated miners and fortune seekers alike. Word spread like the newest mother lode find that citrus could prevent and cure the disease. Demands skyrocketed, and at one time lemons were selling for about $1 each. In today's money that amount equates to about $100 or more.

Typical Southern California cattle ranch owned by immigrants. One of these, Irvine Ranch, evolved into the City of Irvine, now recognized as one of the most desirable places to live in the country.
Courtesy of Corbis Images

Portrait

EUSEBIUS POLLARD 1840 - 1894

Born in Cornwall, England, in 1840, Eusebius Pollard traveled throughout the west and worked in the mining industry before finding his way to the true gold of California: the orange-growing industry. He is remembered as a pioneer exponent of the citrus nursery business and one of the first to raise budded nursery stock oranges in the state. Others remember him as a gifted entrepreneur who invested in real estate, including the subdivision that later became the city of San Marino.

Eusebius's wife, Mary, was born in Truro, England. They were childhood sweethearts who married in Grass Valley, California. She is remembered as a pioneer of Los Angeles County, and she and her husband were charter members of the Methodist Episcopal Church at Alhambra.

Mission records from the earliest times indicate that cattle and fruit production were sporadic. Visitors before 1800 noted that grapes, oranges, apples, pears, plums, figs, pomegranates, peaches, and olives were being cultivated at the missions, but large-scale production was unknown even on the ranchos of Dalton and Reid, as mentioned previously.

The winter of 1861-62 changed the face of farming and agriculture throughout Southern California. It was a flood year; torrential rains devastated the area. The cattle ranchers suffered heavily from the loss of livestock and, never having a solid base, many left the area. The following summer (in 1862) brought drought. Pastures dried to

VIEWS OF DROUGHT

"I well remember the desolation of that year [1864], for I was then a young vaquero on my mother's cattle range in the Suisun Hills. The skies refused their rains: the grasses whitened and withered in the canyons and the high valleys. The cattle starved and died by tens of thousands; beeves [plural of beef] were sold at fifty cents a head. This year may be looked on as marking the decline of the Cattle Era."

—EDWIN MARKHAM OF HIS CHILDHOOD IN CALIFORNIA,
FROM *CALIFORNIA THE WONDERFUL*.

the point of being brittle, and there was no food or water for the grazing cattle or sheep. The crops that did grow shriveled in the fields. The heritage of the great legacy of Mexican cattle ranching was over. As it would do many times throughout the years, the weather in Southern California changed the face of the state.

The new California, which rose from the devastation of tyrannical mother nature, was filled with an energy that has never wavered. In the 1860s the state legislature voted large sums of money to help start other agricultural industries in Southern California. Silk culture began in rural spots such as Los Angeles, Riverside, and San Gabriel, and thousands of mulberry trees were imported and planted.

"California is pre-eminently a silk-producing country. This has passed the experimental stage. The silk industry within her borders is the fabric industry, the fostering of which would give employment to many thousands of women and children who greatly need the money their work would produce, and at the same time keep the many millions of dollars sent to foreign nations in our own country."

—TALIESIN EVANS (THE WELSH BARD AND JOURNALIST),
OVERLAND MONTHLY MAGAZINE, MAY 1893, No. 125.

Tea farms sprang up in Santa Barbara. Coffee plantations were developed near San Bernardino, and there was a push to plant pineapples in San Diego. Fields of cotton were planted near Los Angeles. Castor beans, used for the traditional spring tonic of castor oil, were thought by many to be the next "gold rush" crop and were planted throughout the area. The experiments, for the most part, met with failure, yet cotton and barley succeeded.

It's a little-known fact, but it seems obvious to anyone who has been to or lived in Hollywood on a tropical day: Pineapples and bananas were once cultivated for cash crops in the area that is now Melrose and Sunset.

Working ranches came to be commonplace in early Southern California, and many were owned and run by those from the British Isles. For example, Sphinx Ranch was created in 1879, a 502-acre tract bordering Eaton Canyon in Northeastern Altadena, owned and operated

Orange Pickers. Citrus supported the British Colony in Riverside.
Courtesy of the USC Regional History Collection

by Englishman William Allen. Like other Britishers, Allen came to Southern California for the climate, and named the acreage the Sphinx Ranch since he had spent twenty-three years in Egypt as a broker. During that time he married Emily Bell, the daughter of another British family who had made money in cotton, fruit, and grain. The Allen family consisted of ten children, Annie, Cecil, Edgar, Harold, Walter, Edith, Hubert, Sydney, Percy, and Bernard. Like other British families, the Allens attended the Episcopal Church in San Gabriel and were active in the social scene of the time. The Allen family lived comfortably in a home that had nine spacious rooms on each floor.

The home was a showplace of its time, boasting pantries, a bathroom, lavatories and other "modern" conveniences. An outdoor tennis court was added as the children were ardent fans of that British national pastime.

Originally the ranch had a 50-acre vineyard and a small commercial winery, and Allen added 180 acres in grapes and 26 acres of citrus trees. After the death of Allen, the family continued to run the ranch until the early 1900s, and eventually the ranch was subdivided. When William Allen had purchased the ranch, land sold for $7.50 per acre; in 1925 it sold for $1,800. Today, it's nearly impossible to calculate the cost of an acre in this highly desirable area of Southern California.

At one time there were small groves of oranges planted at the San Gabriel Mission and tended by the priests and Native Americans. Smaller plantings were developed at other missions and on farms around the state, but citrus was a "cottage industry" until the middle

"Grafted and budded trees are being extensively cultivated [in Southern California], the lemon being in all cases the stock. The advantage to be gained from a grafted tree is earlier bearing; but this branch of orange culture is as yet in an experimental state, and the durability of the tree remains to be proved by time. It would thus scarcely be advisable for any one about to enter into this business, with a view of depending upon it for his future livelihood, to run the risk of purchasing this kind of tree, aside from the fact that it might be found inexpedient, for reasons of economy, to pay the extra price they command."

—TALIESIN EVANS, *OVERLAND MONTHLY* MAGAZINE, VOL. 12, MARCH 1874.

of that century, when a vagabond decided to put down roots and seriously cultivate the citrus crop.

The fruits, originally from India, Spain, China, and Algeria, were once a delicacy that only the rich could afford. In ancient Sanskrit the fruits were called *nagrunga* and *nimbu*. Gradually they became known as oranges and lemons.

In 1841, Kentucky wanderer and trapper William Wolfskill settled in what is now Los Angeles. He planted hundreds of seedlings on a two-acre farm at Central Avenue and East Fifth Street. According to Boyle Workman in *The City That Grew*, Wolfskill "also planted the first eucalyptus trees in California." That immigrant tree from Australia seems to typify Southern California even today.

The trees that produced what we call Valencias were then referred to as Mediterranean Sweets. They flourished and Wolfskill expanded his farm to 70 acres. Over a decade the fruit became known as Wolfskill Oranges, noted for their sweetness. The business thrived as Wolfskill and others piled crate loads on board ships heading to San Francisco. By 1875 there were nearly 17,000 of Wolfskill's orange trees thriving in Southern California, yet a middle-age couple from Maine was also in the citrus business and would change the industry again.

Luther and Eliza Tibbets moved to Riverside to avoid the cold winters of the East. The couple linked their heritage to England, and, more importantly, their work in the development of the orange industry produced the British Colony of Riverside. Had it not been for the Tibbetses, the colony would never have come into being.

As a historical side note, history and urban myths intertwine when it comes to the Tibbets's story. One of those is about how Luther Tibbets wrote to the United States Department of Agriculture to gain information on the types of trees to plant around their homestead. He was rewarded by receiving three navel orange trees from Brazil. They are called navels because of the indentation on top of the fruit, which resembles a human navel. Agricultural Commissioner William Saunders, who may or may not have been an intimate friend of Eliza Tibbets, depending on the story one wants to believe, wanted to see if these innovative trees would survive as well as thrive in the balmy Southern California climate.

Two of the three trees not only grew, they flourished. Some historical accounts say that only two trees made the journey from Washington to Riverside; curators of the historical archives in Riverside County say it was three. The Tibbetses of Riverside became famous throughout Southern California for their seedless oranges.

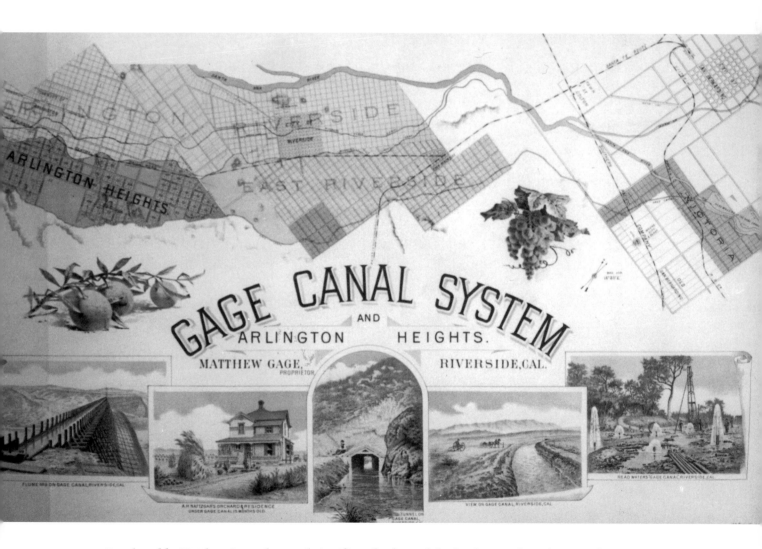

Developed by Matthew Gage, the canal significantly changed the landscape of Southern California.
Courtesy of the Gage Canal Company

The oranges and other crops in the Riverside area, and the entire English colony of Arlington Heights, may have been encouraged by the Tibbetses, but would not have survived without Irishman Matthew Gage, who developed Riverside's extraordinary network of irrigation canals, including the 20-mile waterway named Gage Canal.

Born in Coleraine, Ireland, in 1844, Gage was a rancher, one of the founders of the English colony, and an entrepreneur. He's best remembered for developing the system to irrigate the orange groves and for cultivating relationships with British financial investors, something which had not yet been done.

Matthew Gage induced British investment money into the area. The British financial syndicate, the Riverside Trust Company Ltd., came to California and was later known as the Riverside Orange Company. The Trust bought out Gage and his properties and then developed further canals, and the groves of Arlington Heights blossomed.

At about this time, George Chaffee, Sr., from Kingston, Brockville, Ontario, Canada, moved his son, William Benjamin (called W.B.), and daughter, Emma, to the Riverside area. His wife presumably joined the family later. Chaffee, according to historians, was the first to make irrigation a science.

It's interesting to note that Chaffee's father, Benjamin Chaffee, came from England soon after the War of 1812. He won his greatest fame as an engineer and joint builder of the Victoria Bridge over the St. Lawrence River at Montreal, completed in 1857. Some biographers say that George Chaffee Sr. was self-educated. This seems illogical since his father was a noted engineer. However, regardless of his education or lack of it, he had owned an extremely successful shipping firm that worked on Lake Ontario.

The 2,500-acre tract of land that he purchased was called "Etiwanda," after a Native American chief from the Great Lakes area. Later in life, Chaffee and his family members would set up colonies in Mildura on the Murray River in south central Australia. In his irrigation system, Chaffee installed the first dynamo for the generation of hydroelectric power and, visible for miles around, the first electric light.

George Chaffee, Sr., established the Los Angeles Electric Company and donated the land for the college in Cucamonga that bears his name.
Courtesy of the Ontario Public Library

In 1882, Chaffee established the settlement of Ontario and set acreage aside for an agricultural college. Chaffee College in Cucamonga still bears his name. Chaffee established the Los Angeles Electric Company in 1884 that allowed Los Angeles to become the first city in the United States to be entirely lighted by electric power. He also created a plan to irrigate the desert lands in the Imperial Valley into fertile farm country.

There was a considerable British-based community in the area in the 1890s, and while the land bust gravely affected other areas of Southern California, Riverside maintained a high standard of living. It was, at one time, the richest community in the United States.

Historians in Riverside County point out it was populated by remittance men, second or third sons, and failures from Great Britain looking for colonial opportunities. They found that and more. These were solid, hard-working entrepreneurs such as those working to establish colonies in Argentina, Africa, and Hong Kong at the same time.

Urban myths tend to exaggerate the lives of these citizens, as myths often do, with "talk of ruined peers seeking redemption in the orange groves, but even without such embellishments an intriguing British milieu did take hold in the Arlington Heights district of Riverside," writes historian Kevin Starr, in *Inventing the Dream*.

Regardless of their origins, whether from the British Isles, Canada, or Australia, the colonists upheld English traditions such as afternoon tea (some of the finest were held at the Arlington Heights home of the Gilliland family, much involved in tennis). Traditional sports such as polo and cricket inspired many afternoons spent at the Casa Blanca Tennis Club in the English Colony.

JOURNEY WITH THE SUN
The Pilgrimage of Citrus

They were served with reverence in the Oriental palaces of nabobs and potentates. They occupied places of honor amid rustling silks and the sounds of fountains in the court of Harounal-Raschid. They were known as naranji in the black tents of the Arabs. They delighted dallying King Solomon and the Queen of Sheba.

They were acclaimed beside the Red Sea and within the walls of Jerusalem. Fierce Moors carried them to quench their thirst in the deserts beside the Gates of Hercules. They traveled across the Mediterranean and were piled high on the tables at roman banquets where they were called Arancium. In Spain, Columbus, Queen Isabella, and Cervantes sampled them. Migrating still, at the time of the 1492 discovery of America, they went on a long voyage to the Caribbean, and were carried into Mexico at Vera Cruz.

Up through Mexico they ventured until, at last, they crossed the Sea of Cortez and flourished in Baja California. And then, when the time was right, penetrated into Alta California itself at the moment of Spanish colonization in 1769. Here the stage was being set for their climactic appearance.

—ED AINSWORTH, "THE STORY OF CITRUS IN ITS WESTERN PILGRIMAGE"

Many citrus farms were owned and operated by immigrants from the British Isles.
Courtesy of Corbis Images

"Good land, well-adapted to the cultivation of the orange-tree, can readily be obtained in Los Angeles County, for $25 to $30 an acre."

—TALIESIN EVANS, *OVERLAND MONTHLY MAGAZINE*, VOL. 12, MARCH 1874, No. 3.

Those who are entertained by the detours of research will note that local Riverside County folklore asserts that Eliza Tibbets kept the delicate seedlings alive with dishwater when irrigation water was not available. It is unclear whether Mrs. Tibbets was British or simply traveled in the social circles of the English colony. It is, however, a fact that she modeled her dressing style after royalty, and there's a shocking resemblance between Eliza Tibbets and Queen Victoria.

There is one original navel orange tree, planted in 1872, still standing in Riverside at the home of pioneers Luther and Eliza Tibbets. It can be visited at a small park in Riverside, near Palm and Magnolia Avenues. The world-famous tree, now California State Historical Landmark #20, is tended with care and protected by the most high-tech means to keep it healthy and well.

The bud stock from that tree started the entire wholesale business of the navel orange industry and the cooperative Sunkist that is more than 100 years old.

Local folklore also tells that whenever guests visited the Tibbets's home, platters of newly ripened oranges were passed. It was called the "Washington Navel" then, since the seedlings had come by way of Washington D.C., having originated in South America. The demand for the budded wood with which to propagate more trees was so great that each piece of wood sold for more than $5.

According to records available at the Sunkist archives, most of the navel orange trees (and there are millions) within Southern California originated from the Tibbets's original woodstock.

Early Riverside. Orange groves nestled within the city limits.
Courtesy of the USC Regional History Collection

THE LEGACY OF THE RANCHOS

"At the time of the American conquest of California in 1846…large grants or ranchos were the dominant feature of the province's economic and social life. They remained the controlling factor in much of the state's settlement and agricultural development for many years, and their gradual conversion into cities, towns and farming communities in large measure brought into being the Southern California we know today. The ranchos thus constituted one of the few enduring legacies that California inherited from Mexico and Spain. Two such grants and part of a third went into the making of the Irvine Ranch."

—ROBERT GLASS CLELAND,
THE IRVINE RANCH OF ORANGE COUNTY, 1952.

Yet, if it were not for irrigation and railroad (then later refrigeration cars) the citrus industry would have been a dismal failure, as were the other experimental crops, from pineapples to coffee.

With the completion of the transcontinental railroad, rancher and orange promoter William Wolfskill could now load freight cars full of oranges from his ranch in what is now downtown Los Angeles. In 1877, he sent the first load east to St. Louis. It took more than a month for the freight car to arrive, yet the fruit was still in prime condition. Residents were amazed, and Wolfskill is credited with starting the citrus wholesale marketing industry in California. Navels thrived in the inland valleys; Valencias preferred the coastal strip, especially in Orange County. Lemons grew well in Santa Barbara, Ventura, and San Diego counties.

In 1892, five carloads of California oranges reached London by way of refrigerated railroad cars (a cutting-edge technology of the time) and a 14-day sea voyage in the storage locker of a steamship. Queen Victoria tasted one of the oranges and said it was "palatable." Back in California, Her Highness's comment was good enough to become a ringing endorsement for the fruit that typified Southern California. In this Victorian-fad-seeking area, everyone who considered him or herself of a well-mannered and well-bred nature needed to eat oranges.

For years, citrus was one of the state's only exports. From 1880 to 1893, the citrus acreage grew from just 3,000 acres to more than 40,000. However, growers were hampered to the point of bankruptcy by distribution problems. Farmers would turn their crops over to agents who then sent the fruit to market whether there was a market or not. There were "orange wars," with price fixing and gouging. In 1891, agents insisted that growers take full financial responsibility for the sales, and too many growers netted less than the cost of distribution. They banded together to form a cooperative. The result is the Sunkist Growers, Inc., we know today.

1930 AND NO WATER TO DRINK
Edwin Markham
California the Wonderful, 1914

One labor of Hercules only toughens his fiber and frame for another. So we are not surprised to find that after Los Angeles created her harbor she went on to a new achievement—not surprised to find that she built a mighty aqueduct bringing in a vast supply of water from a mountain lake two-hundred-forty miles away.

In 1905, the city thought that she had provided ample water for generations. But William Mulholland, the water expert, figured out that at the rate her population was increasing there would be a scarcity by 1930. The people were astonished: 1930 and no water to drink! The report was unbelievable: would the expert Mulholland kindly glance again over that page of figures? Yes, verily, it was 1930. But 1930 is only to-morrow on the expanding chart of this city and to-morrow must be provided for immediately.

But while Mulholland figured, Frederick Eaton was winding down out of the mountains with a dream. The world is built by dreams: a dream is the flame-spirit of every great achievement. Mulholland, being a truly practical man, knew the value of dreams; so he had a hospitable ear for the project of Frederick Eaton, the project to tap Owens River in the far mountains and to lead down the abundant waters for the refreshment of the great city.

The two men, dreamer and doer, worked together like the two wings of a soaring bird. Together they sketched out the great labor, and laid the plan before the City Council. There were no grafters in the Council, so they proceeded at once to lay the problem before the people— the need of the water, the deed that would bring it. There being no bosses to beard and no boodler to bully, the town folk were free to talk their own business over and settle it at once. With faith in the future and with the ability to pull together, the people bonded themselves for $23,000,000 to build a channel for the water of the future. Soon the hammers began to sing and the spades to fly.

And now the great labor is finished. The Aqueduct gathers in the sparkling springs that drain Mt. Whitney and other peaks that soar twelve thousand feet in the air. It is a mile high at its fountain-head, and it winds southward along the foothills of the Sierras, then across Mohave Desert and reaches Los Angeles on the level. On it flows through canals, tunnels, covered conduit, siphon, all made of steel and concrete—on it flows—"now it goes sparkling, now it lies darling" on it flows till, reaching the city at last, it delivers its quarter of a billion gallons every twenty-four hours.

The city cannot use all the water now; so the orchard and garden men in the San Fernando Valley are buying water to transform the old grain-fields and cattle ranches into little Edens of flower and leaf.

FATHERING ORANGES

"Having given special attention to the culture and marketing of the Valencia orange, I am often called the 'Father of the Valencia Orange Industry.' I am frequently introduced at a banquet or public gathering as the 'Father of the Valencia Orange,' the chairman or toastmaster not sensing the effect of the omission of the final word. The statement that I was the father of the orange often brought smiles and even laughs among the audience."

—CHARLES C. CHAPMAN, *CHARLES C. CHAPMAN: THE CAREER OF A CREATIVE CALIFORNIA 1853-1944*

ORANGE COUNTY

When California became a state on September 1, 1850, attention was focused on the gold mining in Northern California. But many had been there and decided to move south. Settlers that had come to the fields hearing stories of gold lying atop the ground were too often hungry, hurt, and disillusioned. They left the fields and headed south to Southern California, often thinking that they would eventually make their way again to the East.

Orange County, then part of Los Angeles, was a drought-stricken land. Many ranchers and farmers had to leave. Many of the original Mexican families had lost titles since they were unable to prove ownership to the newly formed state government. The picture was bleak.

Then entered men like Irishman James Irvine who, from success in the grocery business in San Francisco, was able to buy vast parcels of land. In the 1860s, he acquired 120,000 acres, or about one quarter of what is now Orange County, and developed crops of drought-resistant varieties of plants.

Anaheim was the first successful settlement in Orange County; it initially attracted German immigrants. The name Anaheim loosely means "the home next to the Santa Ana River." The Ana comes from Santa Ana and heim comes from the German for home

The first choice was to call the area Richland, because the developers wanted to attract settlers to the rich land. Yet the name Orange County was finally agreed upon by the local lawyers and land developers Andrew Glassell and Alfred Chapman (not related to Charles C. Chapman, who was considered the father of the Valencia orange industry), who were spearheading the project. While we now think of Orange County being named for the fruit, that's not how the name came about. It was named Orange County for a county in Virginia, obviously thousands of miles from the orange groves of Southern California.

JAMES IRVINE
Entrepreneur

"*I* tell you a boy cast upon the world with not a dollar in his pocket, with none within reach…but absolute strangers and without a claim upon any of them is in a position to appreciate the value of a helping hand," said James Irvine. He knew poverty and he knew how to work, and he quickly learned to succeed.

He worked to grow a ranch so large that it was called the Irvine Company and still maintains a presence in Southern California today. His legacy includes vast philanthropic contributions, including the land where the University of California, Irvine, is now.

James Irvine was one of nine children born of Scottish-Irish Presbyterian ancestry. He was of strong, tenacious, God-abiding stock and contributed to the face and future of Southern California in scores of ways. Irvine was born in Belfast, Ireland, on December 27, 1827, and he immigrated to America during the lowest points of the Potato Famine, working as a manual laborer for two years at a paper mill in New York. In 1849 when "gold" was on the tongue of every fortune hunter and vagabond in North America, Irvine and his brother William headed west. In the long and tedious days aboard the ship *Humbolt*, which transported the Irvine brothers to the Isthmus of Panama, they traveled with Dr. Benjamin Flint and Collis P. Huntington, later to become one of the Big Four, who were responsible for the western link of the transcontinental railroad.

Born in Belfast, Ireland, James Irvine's life epitomizes the rags-to-riches dream of immigrants.
Courtesy of the Historical Collection/First American Financial Corporation

The fortune Irvine was to "mine" was not found in the gold fields of Northern California, but in the grocery and produce business when he and others started Irvine & Co. Business was good, and eventually Irvine met and married Nettie Rice. As Irvine would write later about the home they bought in San Francisco on Folsom and Eleventh, the house cost upwards of $25,000, "But it is a very comfortable one with a beautiful yard filled with shrubbery, flowers and clover and there I take solid enjoyment."

Irvine loved California. He would later write, "Flowers bloom here throughout the year in the open air and fresh vegetables in an almost endless variety are to be had in our markets in winter as in summer." He may have been a green grocer by trade, but a farmer and rancher in his soul.

In 1867 Irvine visited the ranches that former shipboard colleague Flint and his partner Bixby had acquired in Southern California, and they became partners, Irvine holding the largest interest. He returned to San Francisco and wrote, "We rode about a good deal, sometimes coming home in the evening after a 30 or 40 miles ride pretty thoroughly tired out, but we had to do it in order to see much of the ranch and the flock." He would acquire nearly one quarter of Orange County.

The weather was cooperative that year and Irvine's holdings soared. With his land secure, he was far from alone.

Irvine Historian Robert Glass Cleland, in *The Irvine Ranch of Orange County*, writes about this time: "Los Angeles and the rich San Gabriel and Santa Ana valleys began to experience one of the first clearly defined real estate booms." Irvine held the lion's share of the county. The factors contributing to the increase in demand were the post-Civil War westward advance of settlements, the completion of the transcontinental railroad, southern families impoverished by the war, and reconstruction.

Cleland continues: "Publicity and advertising, of which California has received a larger share than perhaps any other corner of the globe, were making the state widely known in Europe as well as in the United States and emigrant companies were being organized in Holland, Denmark, Germany and the British Isles to settle in California."

By the late 1880s, the Irvine Ranch had undergone a radical change from grazing and pastoral vastness to farming, which was mirrored by other agricultural changes in Southern

Rotate page to view map.

The Irvine Ranch property stretched to include 22 percent of what is now Orange County.
Courtesy of the Historical Collection/First American Financial Corporation

53

California. James Irvine died in San Francisco in 1886, passing his land holdings and resources on to his heirs. Those same heirs have contributed immensely to the benefit of Southern California, from a university bearing the Irvine name to numerous philanthropic works that have richly benefited people from all walks of life.

Serious researchers and those curious about this Irishman's legacy can access his papers and journals at the Irvine Museum, in Irvine, California.

Historically Speaking

ORANGES?
Let Them Eat Beans.
And They Did.

To the *Chicago Produce News*, October 1911, James Irvine wrote this report about the bean industry on the ranch:

"We have in Limas about 14,000 acres and in black-eyes about 4,000 acres, these acreages forming what is stated both here and in Ventura County to be the largest bean field, *under the one management*, in the world. This land is farmed partly by ourselves and in the greater part by tenants who rent on crop shares. The number of sacks raised on this ranch will approximate 145,000 sacks of Limas and 36,00 blackeyes, or roughly 180,000 sacks of beans which will be worth about $3.50 per sack of 80 lbs. When recleaned or say about $630,000.000.

"We are improving the yield from year to year, owing to better selection of seed and numerous details which lend themselves to successful farming."

Water and Mulholland, Mulholland and Water

Without water, the Southern California area could not have supported a population of more than 200,000. Without water the citrus industry would have failed. Without water, Southern California as we know it today would not have been. Contemporary historians call William Mulholland, "A man obsessed with an engineering challenge of epic proportions," (www.pbs.org), and a man who through a combination of deceit and determination brought water to Southern California.

Mulholland was born in 1878 of modest means in Belfast, Ireland, but even that fact is controversial. Some historical records say he was educated at Christian Brothers' College in Dublin. Others say Cambridge, in England. Some document that he went to sea at age fifteen, which would mean that he didn't attend either university. While the stories are conflicting, the truth is that Mulholland was a determined man, eager for the chance to better his life.

Mulholland's teenage years were spent in lumber camps in Michigan and mining camps in Arizona, where amongst other responsibilities he was hired to fight the Apaches in the southwest. In 1878, the story of water in Los Angeles begins when Mulholland began as a ditch cleaner for a private water company; within eight years the Irishman was the superintendent. When the city of Los Angeles took over the company, Mulholland landed the job as head of the Department of Water and Power, a position he kept until 1928.

These were booming, prosperous years for Southern California. The citrus crops were being shipped throughout the country. The city was growing by hundreds of new residents each day. Small farms, businesses, and oil production, from the Signal Hill and Newhall discoveries, were all on the rise. When Fred Eaton, a one-time mayor of Los Angeles, warned that the city would be faced with a water famine, government officials turned to Mulholland to solve the problem.

He looked north to the Owens River, more than 200 miles away from the city. But there was a conundrum: The newly founded Reclamation Service was in the middle of its Owens Valley irrigation project. Mulholland and Eaton would have to put an end to the project if they wanted the water for Los Angeles. They did. This was a decision that Owens Valley residents would resent for years.

There was considerable argument about the development of the plan. According to an editorial in the *Los Angeles Times*, July 1905, there was a feeling that insiders, knowing that the aqueduct would be brought over the mountains to a point north of the San Fernando Valley, were able to buy land there cheaply from owners unaware of its imminent jump in value. H. J. Whitley, a land developer and friend of Mulholland, owned the lion's share of the valley. Another who prospered was Los Angeles's former mayor and Mulholland friend Fred Eaton. Another may have been owner of the *Los Angeles Times*, Harrison Gray Otis, who was a member of the land syndicate that developed the San Fernando Valley.

"Whoever brings water will bring the people."

—WILLIAM MULHOLLAND, *LOS ANGELES TIMES*, C. 1905.

An Irishman, William Mulholland is best known for bringing water to Los Angeles.
Courtesy of the USC Regional History Collection

In June 1906, Congress passed legislation that let the city of Los Angeles cross federal lands. Through favors given out in their old boys' network, the Federal Reclamation Service extended the national forest boundaries into the Owens Valley, even though the valley's flat regions could hardly be construed as forests. State senators convinced conservationists, including Teddy Roosevelt, to agree to the plan that would benefit Los Angeles "at the expense of the spoliation of lands in the Sierra Nevada," write Julian Nava and Bob Barger in *California: Five Centuries of Cultural Contrast.*

Mulholland designed, supervised the building, and shepherded the project, including the dams and reservoirs; the project began in 1908 and was completed November 6, 1913 when the *Los Angeles Times* head-line shouted: Glorious Mountain River Now Flows to Los Angeles's Gates.

At the celebration as printed by the *Times*, Mulholland said, "This is a great event, fraught with the greatest importance to the future prosperity of this city. I have been already overwhelmed and honored. What greater honor can any man ask than to have the confidence of his neighbors? You have given me an opportunity to create a great public enterprise and I am here to render my account to you.

"It was your own fidelity and unfaltering courage that made the work possible, and I want to thank you. This period in my life is one of great exaltation."

Yet, another historian and civic leader of Los Angeles, Boyle Workman, wrote that Mulholland offered the shortest speech in history, contradicting the speech reported in the *Los Angeles Times*.

"When I was a lad about ten years of age, Mulholland came to Los Angeles, deserting the sea because he wanted to become an engineer. He was a young Irishman, educated at Christian Brothers' College in Dublin."

—BOYLE WORKMAN, *BOYLE WORKMAN'S THE CITY THAT GREW.*

At the opening ceremonies, Workman says, Mulholland stepped forward, pointed to the foaming 150-foot wall of water, and said, "There it is, gentlemen. Take it!"

On the opposite of the water issue and reviewing it with clarity of hindsight, the residents of the Owens Valley were out-maneuvered by Mulholland, Eaton, and others. Mulholland lobbied for the project as if it were a life and death issue for Los Angeles. In reality, much of the water was to be used for irrigating the rich farmlands of the San Fernando Valley, where, incidentally, Mulholland had many business colleagues, and Eaton had quickly purchased land that would sky-rocket when resold to bring through the aqueduct.

After the project was completed, Mulholland's dire predictions that the city couldn't have survived without the water were dismissed or not discussed. During the eight years that it took for the water to be brought to Los Angeles, the population had nearly doubled, but water was still plentiful. However, while the city had enough water without the aqueduct, the San Fernando Valley needed more. Mulholland squeezed water from the Owens River, making millions for his financial backers who held land in the fertile area while bankrupting the farmers of the Owens valley.

What began as a "life-saving mission" for Mulholland and others in Los Angeles turned nasty. On May 21, 1924, dynamite destroyed the Los Angeles Aqueduct. The city offered a $10,000 reward for information leading to the arrest of those behind the act. As the sabotage continued for months, Mulholland received hundreds of threatening letters. His comment? I "half-regretted the demise of so many of the valley's orchard trees, because now there were no longer enough trees to hang all the troublemakers who live there."

No one in Owens Valley breathed a word of who committed the crimes. What began as a nuisance quickly turned to small "accidents" which shortly transformed into the Owens Valley War. An armed California militia was sent to the area to protect the water rights. Tempers flared. Newspaper reporters flocked into Southern California from as far away as Paris to cover the story. The *Times* editorialized that the farmers were "honest, earnest, hardworking American citizens who look upon Los Angeles as an Octopus [referring to the Frank Norris novel of the same name] about to strangle out their lives." It's interesting to note that while the *Times* supported the workers, *Times* founder Otis had profited by the project.

On March 12, 1928, the St. Francis Dam (also called the San Francisquito Canyon Dam in some reference sources) washed away, releasing a 15-billion gallon flood that is known as the greatest civil disaster in contemporary history. The disaster area is located where Magic Mountain is today, near Saugus.

The day after the disaster, the *Times* headline screamed: 200 DEAD, 300 MISSING, $7,000,000 LOSS IN ST. FRANCIS DAM DISASTER.

It happened without warning just three minutes before midnight. The waters, up to 78 feet at some points, swept through the Santa Clara River Valley to the Pacific, about 54 miles away. When it hit Santa Paula, 42 miles south of the dam, the water was 25 feet deep. Livestock, structures, railways, bridges, and orchards and more than 500 people were lost. Damage estimates topped $7 million.

In the inquest, it was found that leaks were seen in the dam and that Mulholland had been at the dam just the day before. He took full responsibility and told the court, "I envy the dead."

The blame rested on Mulholland's shoulders rather than the hands of the Owens Valley River "army," which around kitchen tables and city council chamber offices was continually speculated as being the culprit. Mulholland was put on the stand and admitted that he had noticed nothing out of the ordinary. However, he asserted that leaks were not unusual, especially in dams that size, so those he saw had not caused alarm.

In the end the jury found that the disaster was caused by failure of the rock formations, but Mulholland was to blame, they said. But no criminal charges were brought against him, and he retired shortly thereafter.

He may have been a determined man. He may have been strong-willed and at times accused of being ruthless. He many have done business in a way that even today seems questionable. But when it came to the tragedy at the St. Francis Dam, Mulholland was innocent.

In 1992 an examination of the disaster shed new light on the tragedy and exonerated Mulholland. Using modern technology it was found that there was an ancient landslide in the dam's eastern edge, impossible to detect in the 1920s with the limited scientific skills that existed then.

This Irishman who helped to build the Colorado Aqueduct, Hoover Dam, the Panama Canal, and who brought water to Los Angeles is only honored by a fountain in the Los Feliz area of the city and with a street bearing his name.

Water changed the face of Southern California and ushered incredible economic growth for Los Angeles and the entire lower half of the state.

No, Thanks, No Railroad

Irish immigrant and successful entrepreneur James Irvine was a man of progress, but when it came to Collis P. Huntington's Southern Pacific Railroad, Irvine just said no. And meant it.

Apparently this refusal had nothing to do with the need to ship farm goods north, but had everything to do with a personality clash.

Huntington wanted the right of way to continue the railroad south, connecting Los Angeles with San Diego. The easiest, quickest route was straight through the Irvine Ranch. (Huntington had attempted to avoid confronting Irvine and planned the railroad to be built through Temescal Valley, in Riverside. Unfortunately, floods washed out the tracks.) Irvine refused. This was unusual at a time when land speculators were often just days ahead of the railroad financial agents buying land from unsuspecting farmers in order to make a good profit. Some communities paid the railroad to come through their towns.

Money had nothing to do with Irvine's refusal; it was a personal grudge that started in the 1840s when Huntington and Irvine were aboard the same ship coming to California. There was a disagreement, and as a result, Irvine wouldn't even consider having Huntington's railroad cross his land. When the elder James Irvine passed away, Huntington again took his plea to Irvine's son, James Irvine II. Again, Huntington was told no. Huntington even took his case to Washington, D.C., but Irvine's wishes prevailed.

Not a man to take that word lightly, Huntington was resolute. He wanted to build the railroad across Irvine's ranch. He sent a crew of railroad workers to place the tracks and stop at nothing to do so. "Nothing" came in the form of ranch hands. Irvine called out the men who, with shotguns, dissuaded the railroad workers; accounts have it that they ran off scared for their lives. The railroad workers left, never to return, and some years later, Irvine allowed Huntington's long-time arch-rival, the Atchison, Topeka and Santa Fe, to build through the ranch.

Portrait

THOMAS HOPE

Thomas Hope was a legend in Santa Barbara. As residents and historians know, an area of the county is still called Hope Ranch.

Hope was born in Meath, Ireland, and at age 16, in 1820, he immigrated to America. His travels took him to west Texas and eventually San Francisco, where he married an Irish colleen, Delia Fox. In San Francisco they opened a rooming house and during the gold rush years made and saved enough to sell the property and move to Santa Barbara, working for a fellow Irishman, Nicolas A. Den, whose life is chronicled in Santa Barbara's Royal Rancho, by Walker A. Tompkins.

Hope, uneducated in Ireland, signed all his papers with an "X," yet he was an excellent businessman. Hope acquired 4,000 acres for $8,000 in gold (the standard currency of the time) and then more acreage for just 75 cents an acre. With all his business dealings, he was a farmer at heart, and when ponds or swampy land dried from the occasional drought, Hope quickly put the fields in to barley. With the Civil War raging in the East and price for wool fetching a good return, Hope upped the production of his sheep herds.

Thomas Hope, a devout Catholic, is said to have cared for the displaced and unfortunate Chumash, the local Santa Barbara Native Americans who then came under his care and his employment. While he cared for the less fortunate, he was a fortunate man, one of the richest in the area. His progeny married into families well known in Southern California, including the Suttons. When Hope died in 1876, he had amassed a fortune and firmly engraved his name and personality on the city of Santa Barbara. As a note, Hope died either of stomach cancer or arsenic poison administrated by an enemy.

Modern view of
Hope Ranch in Santa Barbara.
Courtesy of the Photo Collection/Los Angeles Public Library

CHAPTER 3

Influence in Religion

If religious freedom played an early role in Southern California and in the lives of those from the British Isles and Canada, then their socially responsible consciousness was close on its heels.

Reverend Eugene McNamara, introduced in the first chapter, had petitioned the Mexican government for land to settle more than 2000 Irish Catholic families in California. Interest dates back to 1835 when Ireland was in the midst of famine-stricken times, and the full-to-bursting poor of England lived well below any poverty level we can imagine today. It was then that Thomas Coulter told the Royal Geographic Society of London, "California should be considered as a refuge."

Some historians, including Kevin Starr in *Americans and the California Dream 1850-1915*, believe that the Mexican government was pleasantly agreeable to Father McNamara's plan in order to form a "barrier against the invading 'Methodist wolves' of the United

States." Starr writes that although McNamara's scheme never came to anything (and California shortly became part of the United States), a London company anxious to acquire land may have bankrolled it.

While Father McNamara's plan didn't flower, it sprinkled the seeds that those from the Emerald Isle might find religious freedom in California. As Starr writes, "Here on Pacific shores was their promised land, where their long-suppressed culture and Catholicism, their long-starved hunger for land, and their hopes for social dignity and a voice in their own governance might be brought to fruition, safe from British or Yankee repression."

In the 1770s, the Native American religions and rituals began to include Roman Catholicism as a result of the establishment of the missions by Father Junipero Serra, first in 1771 in San Gabriel and then Mission San Fernando in 1779. Although the missionaries enthusiastically converted Native Americans (with history offering differing opinions about how the conversions were effected), religious rites of the tribes were still performed secretly, well off the mission grounds.

Scotsman William Money (later Bishop Money) was the first Protestant minister in Southern California and founded the Reformed Church in 1841. At that time the Catholic clergy called him "the most obstinate heretic on the earth." Yet, California was truly a place for religious freedom, and within a few years, the area boasted a number of small congregations.

"English, in some sense or other of the word, the richest portions of California must become: either Great Britain will introduce her well regulated freedom of all classes and colours, or the people of the United States will inundate the country with their own peculiar mixture of helpless bondage and lawless insubordination."

—SIR GEORGE SIMPSON, OF HUDSON'S BAY COMPANY, FROM *NARRATIVE OF A JOURNEY ROUND THE WORLD, DURING THE YEARS 1841 AND 1842*

As a historical side note, Bishop Money was the first local book author in Los Angeles, publishing *The Reform of the New Testament Church*, in 1854. A self-proclaimed physician, he founded a clinic in Los Angeles and later published a work in Spanish, in which he was fluent, called *A Trieste on the Mysteries of the Physical System and the Methods of Treating Diseases by Proper Remedies*.

The first local Methodist sermon was preached by Rev. James W. Brier in 1850, yet like other small missionary groups, this one moved north, out of the desolation that was Southern California. In 1865 the Episcopal Church came to Los Angeles. The first informal Jewish services had been held earlier, with a formal service in 1862, and that congregation has been ongoing since.

During the land boom of the 1880s, churches sprang up as quickly as communities were built, nearly 40 in the greater Los Angeles area, most of them Protestant. By 1880, 11 denominations had assigned clergy to the area.

Portrait

JOHN J. CROWLEY
The Desert Padre

John J. Crowley was born in Killarney, Ireland, in 1891 and came to the United States with his parents in 1903. Ordained in Massachusetts in 1918, he came to Los Angeles where he served briefly as curate at Saint Agnes Church. He became pastor of mining settlements in Inyo and San Bernardino, where he covered 20,000 square miles serving the needs of his parishioners at the expense of his health.

Father Crowley is best remembered, however, for his work in the Owens Valley. He was determined to bring water to this very dry area. His efforts were successful, culminating in the completion of a dam in 1940. Known as the "Desert Padre," Father Crowley was more than just a beloved monsignor. His commitment to taking care of the material needs of his parishioners resulted in the building of much-needed schools, churches, and hospitals. His concern for the wellness of the whole human being, rather than just the spiritual needs, will be perhaps his most lasting legacy. Father Crowley died in 1940 at the relatively young age of 49. In 1941, Crowley Lake in Mono County was named in his honor.

Father John Crowley is remembered as the Desert Padre.
Courtesy of the Historical Collection/ Los Angeles Public Library

WELSH PRESBYTERIAN CHURCH

The Welsh Presbyterian Church was founded in Los Angeles in 1888 by the Reverend David Hughes and a handful of Welsh immigrants who were anxious to establish a home church for themselves and descendents. An early member was Mary Griffith, sister of Griffith J. Griffith, who donated the land for Griffith Park in Los Angeles.

In 1941, the church choir sang in the Academy Award-winning movie *How Green Was My Valley,* filmed at a re-created Welsh village in Santa Monica.

By the beginning of the twentieth century, Protestant evangelism had come to Southern California. There were more than 231 Christian churches with a membership estimated at over 80,000. According to historians Leonard Pitt and Dale Pitt, "The proliferation of religious sects in the early part of the century was attributed to the hospitable climate, the presence of many uprooted and alienated émigrés, and the host of wealthy, leisured individuals arriving from all parts of the globe." It is important to remember that along with these transplants came people who believed in diverse spirituality, such as fortune-tellers, astrologers, occultists, swamis, and psychics.

In the countryside far from the cities of Riverside and Los Angeles, churches were taking root. In San Gabriel, for instance, the

Church of Our Savior (part of the Episcopal diocese of Los Angeles, which had begun services already) began in the summer of 1864, when services were held by the Rev. Mr. D. O. Kelley and then later by the Rev. Dr. Henry Messenger. It was the only non-Roman Catholic group in the valley, and from the very beginning, worshipers of various Protestant faiths came. Today the connection to the British Isles continues with Welshman Dr. Gethin V. Hughes holding the position of Bishop for the Episcopal Dioceses in San Diego.

Contrary to the picture of blooming Christianity in early Southern California, things could be pretty bleak and tedious in the quest to attend services. As with other segments of life, one had to be determined. For instance just to travel to the Episcopal Church, the organist, Mrs. Peck, had to drive in a lumber wagon drawn by an old mare and a mule. The trip took more than two hours one way.

Historically Speaking

[Santa Barbara was] "an unprogressive town, with no telegraph or railroad, although they had a daily stage to Los Angeles and a steamship to San Francisco every four days. The present Church capacity of the community, including the old mission, would accommodate every man, woman and child in the place, leaving room for several hundred more."

—EPISCOPAL BISHOP KIP, WHO WROTE IN HIS JOURNAL OF FEBRUARY 13, 1870.

The Rev. Mr. Archibald G. L. Trew was an Episcopalian from Quebec, Canada. The Rev. Trew, according to historical accounts, had been lucky to be alive when he left Canada on a stretcher. He was, most people believed, hopelessly ill with tuberculosis and not expected even to reach California alive. While others thought he was handicapped, the Rev. Mr. Trew got to work. Within two year's time, he had built the parish up so strongly that the mortgage was paid off and the church was free of debt. In that time, he also established churches in Duarte, Sierra Madre, and East Los Angeles. He became the Dean of St. Paul's Cathedral in Los Angeles.

Several denominations grew locally during this time including the Church of the Nazarene, the Pentecostal Movement, the Hebrew Evangelization Society, and the Christian Fundamentals League. Another splinter group was the Foursquare Gospel Movement created by Aimee Semple McPherson, born in Ontario, Canada, of British immigrants. McPherson, charismatic and popular with a flamboyant view of preaching the gospel, constantly fought off enraged Protestant ministers with her unorthodox style in public forums and on the radio. Yet, few protest how she helped the poor during the Great Depression. Her son, Rolf, is still active in the work of her Four Square Gospel Churches.

Reverend Archibald Trew established several Episcopalian congregations in the San Gabriel and Los Angeles areas.
Courtesy of the Episcopal Diocese of Los Angeles

Portrait

WHEN HOLLYWOOD AND RELIGION MIXED
The Evangelical Superstar, Aimee Semple McPherson

*B*orn in Canada of British immigrant parents, but remembered most in Los Angeles, the Reverend Aimee Semple McPherson may be one of Southern California's most flamboyant religious leaders. During her life, 1890-1944, the Rev. McPherson founded the fundamentalist Foursquare Gospel Church.

Historical sources suggest that there was nothing ordinary about the minister. She was a convert to Pentecostalism and lived for a time in China with her missionary husband, who died during their stay there. The union with Harold S. McPherson, her second husband, ended in divorce. At 26 she began a career as a tent revivalist.

When she and her sick child arrived in Los Angeles, the city was aflutter with cutting-edge technology and the glitz and glamour of the movie industry taking hold. Additionally, the First World War casualty list was growing by the day. The ordinary citizen was anxious for new voices, and "Sister" shared hope along with the gospel, faith healing, and flash that was not known in other religious services in the area.

Within five years of making her home in Los Angeles, McPherson had built and dedicated Angelus Temple, which could seat more than 5,000. Services routinely were at capacity. The temple, costing $1.5 million, was funded by donations and was located in Los Angeles's Echo Park area.

The Foursquare Gospel is based on the concepts of the Savior, baptism, healing, and the Second Coming. But Aimee Semple McPherson was no conservative minister, she was a show-business-style, flashy preacher. Local press accused her of conducting "religious vaudeville" spectacles. Yet her congregation adored her.

She was beautiful, blond, young, and vibrant, and she acquired an enormous following. Sister typically dressed in white flowing gowns and carried small bouquets of flowers. At one time her church had more than 4,000 branches, a radio studio, and worldwide missions.

But all wasn't perfect in the world of Aimee Semple McPherson. She suffered from depression and perhaps even from too much exposure to her beloved public and followers.

Canadian born Aimee Semple McPherson is best remembered for her
generosity during the bleak years of the Great Depression.

There's still a mystery surrounding her kidnapping, and many wonder if it was a hoax, arranged as a PR stunt, or if it really happened.

On May 18, 1926, Los Angeles woke to the news that Sister had been abducted while she'd been swimming at the beach on the coastline of Venice, California. Followers flocked to the shore and some combed the sand for any sign of evidence. One follower drowned and another died of exposure in the hunt for her abductors.

A ransom note appeared, signed "The Avengers," and demanded $500,000 for Sister's safe return. After 32 days of futile investigations and countless police searches, Sister Aimee stumbled out of the desert, near Douglas, Arizona, claiming that she'd been kidnapped, tortured, drugged, and held by the Avengers in a shack in Mexico. She told the press that her abductors had been careless and she'd escaped, walking 13 hours before reaching help.

However, she didn't look like someone who had been abused. Her shoes showed no wear from the 13-hour hike and she couldn't lead authorities to the shack in Mexico. She could give no good reason as to how she could disappear wearing a swimsuit and turn up fully dressed (including her corset) a month later.

Yet, there had been threats against Sister's life the month before and a foiled kidnapping scheme in September 1925. Rumors flew around the city. Some said she was having an illicit affair. Other "insiders," who purportedly knew Sister well and wanted to reveal "the truth," spread rumors about how she'd had an abortion. Some people insisted that she was having a facelift or recovering from surgery. One story is that she was hiding out with her lover in the Hollywood Hills during the entire time that she was supposedly missing.

A Los Angeles district attorney charged her with perjury, but Sister Aimee stuck with her story and the charges were dropped. The faithful and the curious still flocked to the Angelus Temple throughout the ordeal, and the mystery has never been solved.

The story of Aimee Semple McPherson ends on a sad note. After a few more years of preaching and lecturing internationally, the press's love affair with the minister fizzled, and she became despondent, dying of a drug overdose in 1944. The Foursquare Gospel Church, however, still has more than two million members worldwide, and the headquarters in downtown Los Angeles, near Echo Park, are the subject of a discussion on renovation.

Working together for the good of their hometown and surrounding area Methodists, Baptists, Presbyterians, and others—except for Spiritualists—contributed money and labor to build a community church. The first church in Riverside stood on the northwest corner of Sixth and Vine Streets.

Reverend Roger A. O'Shea, a native of County Kerry, Ireland, received his preliminary educational training at a parochial school at Ballybunnion, attended St. Brendan's at Killarney, and St. Patrick's at Carlow before crossing the Atlantic to Toronto, Canada. He came to Los Angeles in 1916. He was part of the clergy for the Catholic Church in Southern California, and he was pastor of Los Angeles's St. Anselm's in the 1900s. An activist, he is considered by his biographers to be instrumental in helping the community in education and religious programs. In 1905 the parish house, then located on 34th Street, had five classrooms, a large auditorium and a music room. There were five sisters of St. Joseph as teachers to the nearly 300 students.

One of the pioneers of religion in the Riverside area and the new Colony, was the Right Rev. Msgr. Thomas J. Fitzgerald, V.F., pastor of the Scared Heart Parish, Redlands. When Father Fitzgerald, originally from County Kerry, Ireland (with a brief sojourn to Scotland), came to the area, there was only a handful of Anglo-Catholics. "This did not deter the ambitious young clergyman who took delight in the landscape of Riverside county and declared it to be the most beautiful place he had ever seen. Despite the lack of prospects he vowed to build a church there," writes Patrick J. Dowling, in *Irish Californians*.

In 1892 both the priest and the people wanted a church, although most all the citizens were suffering from the bust of the land boom. While the area didn't suffer from the land bust as much as other regions, economic times were tight.

One citizen remarked, "Father, you are very foolish to build a church in Redlands. You cannot do it." To that Father Fitzgerald replied, "If you are as sure of going to Heaven as I am to build a church in Redlands you are a lucky man." The priest was a man of his word, and on that day in 1895 when the roof was put on the church, he accepted a tidy check from this skeptic.

Father Fitzgerald traveled the countryside by horse and buggy from Beaumont to Redlands to say Mass and minister to the sick and dying. For more than two years, he came by freight train (thanks to Huntington's Southern Pacific Railroad) to visit the communities.

By the 1920s the Los Angeles mid-Wilshire district (named for flamboyant entrepreneur H. Gaylord Wilshire, of British descent) was crowded with houses of worship with the largest and wealthiest preferring the Gothic design style.

Born in County Kerry, Ireland, Rev. Msgr. Thomas Fitzgerald, V.F., was Founder and Pastor of Sacred Heart Parish, Redlands, California from 1857-1930.
Courtesy of the Patrick Dowling Family

Sister Aimee's Angelus Temple
still stands near Echo Park.
Courtesy of the USC Regional History Collection

CHAPTER 4

Influence in Education

Along with the ranchers, farmers, and those seeking health cures, came people associated with commerce and industry. They all needed more, and thus came their determination to provide schools and higher education for Southern California's children. Those from the British Isles and Canada were instrumental in this developmental stage, too.

Before the twentieth century, education was primarily a local affair, often run through churches and parochial schools. Although public education was mandated by the state constitution in 1850, schools were few. In the early days circa 1849, the only teachers in Los Angeles, for example, were private tutors. The first school in Southern California supported by public funds, School No. 1, was built between 1854 and 1855 and located on 2nd and Spring Streets in Los Angeles. Father Thomas J. Fitzgerald, of Redlands (originally from County Kerry, Ireland), was an enthusiastic supporter of education for all children.

As Patrick Dowling writes in *Irish Californians*, "One of Father Fitzgerald's pet projects was the establishment of a parochial day school for local Catholics who could not afford the cost of young students living away from home."

Father Fitzgerald believed, "No matter how grand and beautiful a church may be, how large and well-ordered the Sunday School it may have, how elegant the parochial mansion, a parish without a school is incomplete. A school is the nursery of the church." Within two years of making this statement the school was finished.

With the land boom and immigration to "California the Wonderful," as Edwin Markham titled it, educational opportunities in Southern California mushroomed. Private schools were the educational choice for well-to-do families, who also patronized exclusive college-prep institutions that taught the basics, as well as painting, languages, and physical education. Higher education changed, too, with more local colleges and universities gaining recognition.

For instance, Los Angeles's University of Southern California was co-founded by former California Governor John G. Downey, an Irish-Catholic businessman. James Irvine began the legacy of prosperity in Orange County, and his heirs gave land on which to build the University of California, Irvine, known throughout the world. London-born Ellen Browning Scripps devoted her life and fortune to pioneer an innovative college for women, now Scripps College in Claremont.

Not all education was on the higher level, though, especially in the beginnings of the state. From 1856 to 1862 Charles Hardy, a native of

LAND BOOM
Tales from the Front

"Extraordinary situations arose out of the speculative mania, as when over-ambitious folks, fearful perhaps least they might be unable to obtain corner- and other desirable-situated lots, stationed themselves in line two or three days before the date of anticipated land-sales…twenty or more optimistic of our boomers would often have two or three substitutes waiting in a line extending irregularly far down the sidewalk and assuming at night the appearance of a bivouac.

"I have heard it said that as much as a hundred dollars would be paid to each of these messengers, and that the purchaser of such service, apprehensive lest he might be sold out, would visit his representative many times before the eventful day.

"Later this system was improved and official placement numbers were given, thus permitting people to conduct their negotiations without much loss of time."

—HARRIS NEWMARK, *SIXTY YEARS IN SOUTHERN CALIFORNIA*

England, taught a small group of children at the home of Louis Robidoux, in the Riverside area. He said that he received $50 a month from the state (presumably through the local San Salvador District) and $15 per month plus board and room from Mr. Robidoux. Then the new Riverside School District built a bungalow to house its students, including those from the British and Irish families in the colony. The building was just 16 by 24 feet, located on Sixth Street between what is now Lime and Mulberry. The cost of the building was $1,300—a fortune at that time.

Ellen Browning Scripps

ELLEN BROWNING SCRIPPS

Ellen Browning Scripps might be one of the most remarkable women who ever attended Scripps College. She founded it. The college was originally known as Scripps College for Girls. Ms. Scripps dedicated her dreams as well as her resources to pioneering an innovative setting for a special learning place suited for women. At ninety years of age, she still saw life in terms of possibility and spoke of the women's college that opened its doors in 1926 as her new adventure.

Philanthropist and newspaper entrepreneur, Ellen Browning Scripps, born in London, England October 18, 1836, was educated at Knox College in Galesburg, Illinois, before becoming a teacher and later joining her Londoner brother, E. W. Scripps (journalist and newspaper tycoon) on his ranch in Miramar, near San Diego. Later she built South Molton Villa in La Jolla, named for her father's bindery address in London.

Ms. Scripps had a deep and practical interest in the welfare and education of children and young women. In addition to the college in Claremont, California, during her life she graciously donated funds to build children's playgrounds, founded clubs, contributed to the La Jolla library and to the building of St. James Church, the Bishop's School, and a pool for children at the La Jolla breakwater.

"The paramount obligation of a college is to develop in its students the ability to think clearly and independently, and the ability to live confidently, courageously and hopefully," said Ellen Browning Scripps. And her dream continues at the outstanding women's college that bears her name.

Ellen Browning Scripps spearheaded education for women.
Courtesy of the USC Regional History Collection

A College Comes to Town

In 1879 three community leaders in Southern California, Ozro W. Childs, a Protestant horticulturist; former California Governor and native of Ireland, John G. Downey; and Isaias W. Hellman, a German-Jewish banker and philanthropist, deeded 308 lots to the Board of Trustees of the promising University of Southern California. The lots were located in what was designated West Los Angeles, near the intersection of Vermont Avenue and Exposition Boulevard. The sales of the lots were to create an endowment that would seed the university.

The University of Southern California opened in 1880 with 53 students and 10 teachers. The university struggled for financial balance in the rapidly expanding community. While other universities, such as Northern California's Stanford University, thrived on the generous contributions of benefactors, USC forged ahead on the energies of faculty, deans, presidents, and trustees.

University of Southern California Bovard Administration Building, designed by architect, John Parkinson.
Courtesy of the Parkinson Archives

Portrait

John Gately Downey

JOHN GATELY DOWNEY

A druggist by profession and community leader in Southern California, Irish-born John Gately Downey became governor of California in 1859. His rags-to-riches story mirrors many of the immigrants from the British Isles and Canada. Today his legacy includes a Southern California city bearing his name.

Downey arrived in Los Angeles, a bedraggled boy of 15, during the gold rush years. Much like Irvine and others, the poverty and chancy life of gold fields quickly lost their luster. In time, the self-educated Downey owned the only drugstore between San Diego and San Francisco.

Downey was elected lieutenant governor on the Democratic ticket at age 32, and then was appointed governor and served in that office from 1860 to 1862. He was the first Southern Californian to achieve that high an office.

Although he was a Union supporter, many perceived him as a Confederate sympathizer and he wasn't reelected. Downey was a business leader and entrepreneur. His diverse enterprises included his drugstore, land (Warner's Ranch and the Santa Gertrudis Rancho, which he subdivided and established as the town of Downey), real estate (called the Downey Block, on Temple and Spring Streets in Los Angeles, and the subdivisions of Norwalk and Santa Fe Springs), and banking. The Downey Block was the site of Los Angeles's first public library.

Irish born John Gately Downey co-founded USC and was the first California governor elected from the southern part of the state.
Courtesy of the Downey Historical Society

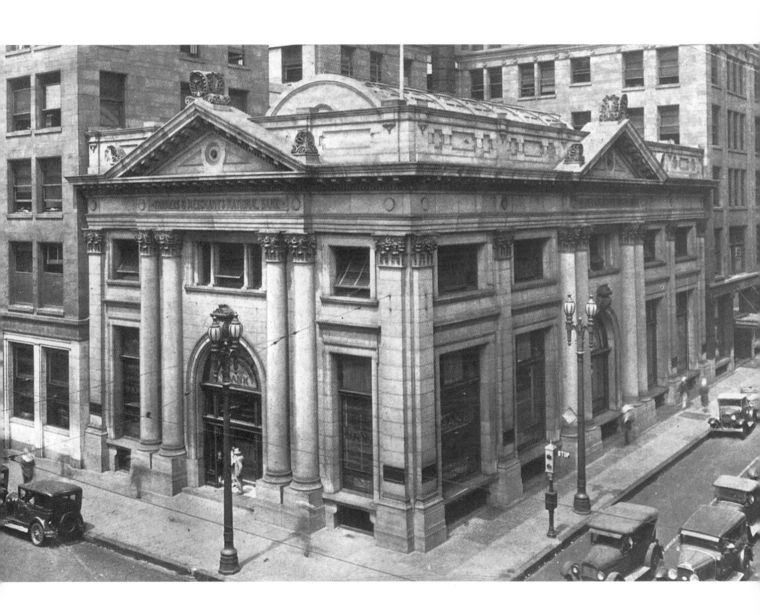

Farmers and Merchants Bank,
co-founded by Irishman, John Gately Downey.
Courtesy of the Photo Collection/Los Angeles Public Library

Downey joined business forces with Alvinza Hayward, the richest man in California (who staked a mine during the gold rush that produced more than $25 million), and I. W. Hellman, who was in the banking business. Downey and Hellman founded Farmers and Merchants Bank of Los Angeles, established in 1871. This later became Security Pacific Bank, which in 1993 merged with Bank of America.

Historian Kevin Starr writes that Downey "promoted public improvements: a railroad connection with San Francisco, horse-drawn streetcars for Los Angeles in 1873, a public library system, the chamber of commerce (originally known as the Board of Trade), the University of Southern California, and the historical society."

In 1868, Downey and Dr. John Strother Griffin, a physician and fellow entrepreneur, founded the Los Angeles City Water Company. In 1873, they constructed and laid iron water pipes through East Los Angeles. Downey would eventually hire William Mulholland, a fellow Irishman, to bring water to Southern California.

Historically Speaking

THE USC "METHODISTS"

No, you won't find the USC Methodists in any of the PAC 10 football games. In 1912, USC's feisty athletic teams, originally known as the Methodists, were renamed the Trojans. *Los Angeles Times* sports reporter Owen Bird wrote that USC athletes at a track meet "fought like Trojans." The name stuck and the campus "Tommy Trojan" statue was unveiled on June 6, 1930.

"The University of California, Berkeley, has always leaned toward the practical as well as toward the classical, never failing to favor courses in mining and engineering. And one of the most heartening facts in the advancing life of the State is the living interest the University is taking in the work of the folk of field and orchard.

"The Agricultural College reaches down to the ground: it instructs not only University students in the classroom and in laboratory, but it also goes out to instruct high-school students and to give light to the field-workers looking for light. It has experiment stations in Riverside and Imperial Valley, a pathological laboratory at Whittier, and forestry stations in the north and in the south.

"Thus the college is a center of light and joy; for the instructed farmer not only has more power but also more happiness. The University also extends its kindly hand into the home. Household science is taught to the mothers and daughters, and stress is laid upon conditions that are right for children, and also upon the knowledge that will tend to sweeten the days and lift the load of the farmer's wife."

—EDWIN MARKHAM, *CALIFORNIA THE WONDERFUL*, 1914.

Opening Day for City Hall in 1928.
Designed by John Parkinson.
Courtesy of the Parkinson Archives

CHAPTER 5

Influence in Architecture

$\mathcal{S}$outhern California has always been a mecca for innovative styles and powerful changes in architecture.

While many of the names and incidents may not instantly be familiar, you'll clearly understand the importance of their inclusion and the legacy they have established.

The Architecture Begins

What we see in Southern California today, the skyscrapers of Los Angeles; the stately homes in Pasadena, Altadena, San Diego, Riverside, Redlands, and other communities, would be absent from the landscape if it were not for the influence of people from the British Isles and Canada.

English immigrant and architect John Parkinson helped design Los Angeles's "face." His architectural firm, begun in 1888, recently celebrated its 107th year, with offices in Los Angeles and Austin, Texas. William Scott Field, AIA, principal of the firm and president of the Parkinson archives explains: "There are many projects that JP, as his friends called him, must have been proud of. The Los Angeles City Hall; USC campus; Federal Building; the department store known as Bullock's-Wilshire, [a] building designed with the help of his son, Donald; Union Station; the Braly Building on 4th and Spring; and the Coliseum are a few."

Portrait

JOHN PARKINSON
Inventor and Architect

John Parkinson (JP to his friends), built fences in Winnipeg and stairs in Minneapolis. He attended night school to learn drafting. He had the mind and heart of an inventor and attempted to devise elevators that would be effective. He is one of the best-known and most visible architects in Southern California. Much of his work seems to announce to any tourist that they've "arrived" in this state.

Even today, you can tour Los Angeles and see his designs come to life in the Los Angeles City Hall, much of the old USC campus, the Los Angeles Memorial Coliseum and its rose garden, and Amtrak's Union Station, amongst others.

Born in Scorton, a small village in Lancashire County, England, in 1861, he was apprenticed for six years to a contractor/builder near Bolton, England. His biographers explain that this was where he gained his practical knowledge and honed the construction skills that would set his work apart.

At 21 he left England for the adventure of America, yet he returned to his native land shortly thereafter, only to find out that in order to advance in the building trades of England, he would have to put in much more time. According to biographer William Scott Field, AIA, curator of the Parkinson archives and current principal of Parkinson Field Associates, Architects, "His first ten years in Los Angeles were a monetary struggle. He did sell some of his elevator patents to Otis Elevator. In his letters and journals, JP noted that he gave up trying to invent, then just stuck to architecture from 1904 on. It is here, of course, where he excelled."

The president of the University of Southern California (which was originally founded by a group that included Irishman John Downey), contacted John Parkinson to develop the school's master plan. By this time Parkinson had established himself as the leading architect in Southern California, and he had experience in educational settings. Parkinson had designed the Manual Arts High School campus in 1910. The USC buildings he designed were

One of the most noted architects in Southern California was Britisher John Parkinson.
Courtesy of the Parkinson Archives

impressive brick and stone structures in the Lombard Romanesque Revival style. Even more buildings were planned for the USC campus (but never realized), and all were designed by Parkinson and his firm.

Amtrak's Union Station, another of Parkinson's designs, is an example of the blending of Spanish Colonial Revival Style and what is known today as Streamline Modern, representing the machine-age aesthetic. Los Angeles City Hall is probably the best-known symbol of architecture in Southern California.

Saint Athanasius Episcopal Church was one of the earliest brick buildings constructed in Los Angeles (1864). It was built at the foot of "Poundcake Hill," the intersection of Temple and

New High Streets. It was sold to the city in 1883 so that a new courthouse could be built. Today the current City Hall stands on the site.

An early design from the Parkinson archives shows a short, stubby building that would conform to the city's code of keeping buildings less than 150 feet tall. The city council decided to change its own rules in order to make City Hall stand as a symbol and be the tallest structure around. Thus came to be the axiom that "a municipality is not governed by its own ordinances." City Hall is a blend of Classical and Mediterranean, with a Modern flair. In 1986 Project Restore undertook the restoration of the city's symbol to its 1928 glory.

The Memorial Coliseum was funded by a private group of newspaper publishers, and they retained Parkinson. Their goal? To attract the 1924 Olympic Games, and while the International Committee didn't select the site, the plans were completed and USC proposed to hold its football games there. Critics said that the backers would never be able to fill the stands. Would 75,000 people really come for a football game? Most doubted it.

In 1932 Los Angeles was able to attract the Olympic games to the city and the Parkinsons (now father and son working together) were contracted again. They were asked to enhance the facility with an addition of 35,000 seats.

St. Athanasius Church was one of the earliest buildings in Los Angeles. City Hall occupies this site today.
Courtesy of the Photo Collection/Los Angeles Public Library

Los Angeles Coliseum during the 1932 Olympics. Designed by John Parkinson.
Courtesy of the Parkinson Archives

In Southern California Parkinson designed the cutting-edge buildings of the time, including the first skyscraper in 1904, which was called the Braly Block, on 4th and Spring. It was hailed in newspapers as a technological achievement. It was thoroughly modern for the time and included "devices" that were groundbreaking. These included controlled steam heat, incandescent lighting, internal vacuum cleaning systems, electricity, piped gas for medical offices, porcelain lavatories, and telephone, telegraph, and message wires in every office. There were three elevators for the safest vertical travel in the country. It held the distinction of being the tallest building (173 feet tall) in Los Angeles, until Parkinson's City Hall, rising to 450 feet, was completed in 1928. Parkinson collaborated with fellow Englishman John C. Austin on the Braly Block, and it's interesting to note that Austin went on to design the Griffith Park Observatory.

OLVERA STREET
Dreams Become Reality

Once it was a small, clustered, crowded substation for the Big Red Cars, Los Angeles's electric trolley system. Then neglect fell upon Olvera Street, and many forgot that it was the site of the Avila Adobe and other historic buildings constructed by the city's former mayor, Francisco Avila, in 1818. The Pelanconi House, the oldest brick house in the city, c. 1855, and the Sepulveda House, c. 1887, were there, too. Back then it was called Wine Street, a short lane in the middle of the city.

After the land boom and subsequent depression struck Southern California, even this historic spot took a hit. When Christine Sterling, a champion of the arts and architecture in Los Angeles, walked through the plaza and streets in 1926, she was shocked by what she saw: dilapidated buildings lying in ruin. Sterling began to seek out funding to renovate the area, and with publicity from the *Los Angeles Times* and influential city pioneers, the dream began to come true. Those who offered to donate funds to cover the costs of materials were Harry Chandler; Henry O'Melveny, a prominent Irish attorney and pioneer in Los Angeles; Lucien N. Brunswig, president of Brunswig Drug Company; James R. Martin, a banker; General Moses H. Sherman, owner of the Los Angeles Electric Railway Company; and Rudolfo Montes, who later started the Port Authority in New Orleans.

Descendants of the Avila family encouraged Sterling to continue the refurbishment, and with her untiring effort the project took hold. The city council closed Olvera Street to cars in 1929. Sterling received help from the city's Department of Water and Power, which drew up plans to grade the street. The sheriff's department provided prisoners to do the labor. Mrs. Sterling recorded in her diary, "Every day I pray that [the sheriff] will arrest a bricklayer and a plumber."

Today one can see where the original *Zanja Madre* (or mother ditch) was located in the pueblo, with its pathway marked in the street by diagonal brickwork.

Trees were planted and a large cross was erected at the south end of Olvera Street. The Mexican market place was officially opened on Easter Sunday, April 20, 1930, to "preserve and present the customs and trades of early California." La Golondrina Café, opened on Olvera Street in 1930, was the first restaurant in the downtown Los Angeles area to serve authentic Mexican food.

"Olvera Street holds for me all the charm and beauty which I dreamed for it, because out of the hearts of the Mexican people is spun the gold of Romance and Contentment. No sweeter, finer people live, than the men and women of Mexico and whatever evil anyone believes about them has been bred in the darkness of ignorance and prejudice."

—Mrs. Christine Sterling, patron and manager of the historic plaza at Olvera Street, Los Angeles, in her journal entry of April 19, 1930.

Los Angeles's Union Station was designed by John Parkinson.
Courtesy of the Parkinson Archives

Architectural styles from the time that gold was discovered in 1848 at Sutter's Mill to the end of World War II teach any observer just how swiftly tastes change. Southern California went from adobe homes, often without floorboards, to the grand mansions of the ranchos, created by the likes of British subjects Dalton and Reid, to the Yankee- and English-style wood and fired-clay brick. This all took place in less than one hundred years.

Materials were scarce; entrepreneurs snatched wood off boats in the San Pedro and San Diego harbors and sold it to the highest bidders. Lumber had to be imported from the Pacific Northwest and the Mendocino coast. Between the 1860s and 1870s buildings were a montage of styles: Greek Revival, Italianate, Eastlake, Romanesque, Shingle, Queen Ann, and Colonial Revival. The towns in Southern California, historians like to point out, looked much like Cleveland, St. Louis, and Milwaukee. This occurred, of course, because those who had learned the building trades were from these cities. These were the land boom days when thousands were being lured to Southern California.

Yet, architecture and progress do not stand still. The first steel-reinforced, fireproof building in Southern California was the Homer Laughlin Building (owned by Homer Laughlin, of Scottish-Irish ancestry and founder of the pottery business that produced the popular ceramic Fiesta Ware). The building was designed by John Parkinson and was considered to be at the height of innovative technology and architecture.

"This is no mining boom, based upon ledges that can be pinched out or worked out. This is no oil boom, based upon a product the supply of which can readily exceed the demand. This is no boom based upon wheat deals, or pork corners, or financial deadfalls, or railway combinations, or other devices of man. This boom is based upon the simple fact that hereabouts the good Lord has created conditions of climate and health and beauty such as can be found nowhere else, in this land or any land, and until every acre of this earthly paradise, the influx will continue."

—*San Diego Union*, October 1, 1887.

Changes in architectural styles came quickly at the turn of the twentieth century. Southern California was luring droves of people and homebuilders, eager to subdivide and make money. There was plenty of land to be had, even though water was a worry to many communities. This concern prompted the city planners in Los Angeles to appoint Irishman William Mulholland to solve this calamity. As described in chapter 2, it was decided that water would be diverted from the Owens River to keep Los Angeles and the vicinity from dying of thirst. The entire project is considered an engineering and architectural feat for its time.

A notable introduction into the scheme of building was the bungalow. It originated in Asia but was adapted and loved by middle-class families who were moving to Southern California to avoid the harsh winters of the East. The bungalow was also popular among those who later moved to Southern California for the war effort and aviation industries. The bungalow was part of the Arts and Crafts, or Craftsman movement, and was popular and influential in the beginning of the twentieth century.

A descendant of early English immigrants who settled on the East Coast, Henry E. Huntington is best known today for his generous spirit with the gifts of art, literature, historical records, and botanical collections at his former estate, which is now the Huntington Library and Art Gallery in San Marino. The fabulous collection contains Gainsborough's Blue Boy and a Guttenberg Bible, amongst other priceless pieces of art and books. The gardens at the estate were a source of pleasure for Huntington and his family. Today there is a 12-acre desert garden, which is in spectacular bloom in the spring, a 6-acre Japanese garden, a palm garden, and a Shakespeare garden.

James Thorpe, in *Henry Edwards Huntington: A Brief Biography*, writes, "Huntington made a good deal of money…but he never tired to maximize his profits. He was a lover of Southern California before he was a businessman. Huntington said, 'I could have made a whole lot more money out of this country than I have done, if money-making had not been tempered with real affection for this region.'"

The Mission Revival architectural style influenced many architects and builders. The most readily accessible example of this style can be seen today in Riverside's famous Mission Inn, popular because it captured the romance of Helen Hunt Jackson's *Ramona*. (It is thought

"This is an era of town building in Southern California, and it is proper that it should be so, for the people are coming to us from the East and from the North and from beyond the sea and for the great multitude whose faces are turned with longing eyes toward this summer land and who will want homes among us, we must provide places. And while there is much room in Pasadena and in Monrovia and in other pleasant towns, yet Pasadena prices, and even Monrovia prices are rather high for the purses of many who will come, and these places are rapidly filling, and the prices are getting higher."

—*PASADENA DAILY UNION*, SEPTEMBER 5, 1887.

that Jackson modeled the story after the life of the "Scotch Paisano" Hugo Reid and his bride, Victoria.)

The Mission Revival movement blossomed in the Inland Empire as an architectural and decorative style with literary overtones. The man who did most to excite the well-heeled public and the middle-brow citizens for the movement was Charles Fletcher Lummis, a colorful, flamboyant New Englander who became a noted author, naturalist, and editor of the *Los Angeles Times*.

The Mission Revival styled flowed out of the Riverside area and to all of Southern California. It was adopted for city halls, homes, churches, and railroad stations. For a while it was seen on storefronts, too. Not to be confused with the earlier period, sometimes called Hispanic or Spanish Traditional, Mission Revival features the plain surfaces and elaborate ornamentation of the early missions.

IS IT ECHO PARK? OR DERBYSHIRE?

*E*cho Park, known throughout Southern California, is actually a replica of Derbyshire, England, at least in the mind of its designer.

Long before it was part of Los Angeles's crowded city center, it was a lush, small valley area with a natural spring-fed stream. In 1868, the Los Angeles Canal and Reservoir Company dammed the arroyo to make a reservoir that aided in powering a woolen mill at what is now 6th and Figueroa (then called Pearl Street). It served local residents with water and irrigated the walnut and orange groves, including those planted by William Wolfskill that dotted "downtown" Los Angeles and the pueblo areas. Immigrants, many coming from the British Isles and Canada to work in the mills and help build the city, began to settle in the area.

When the mill closed in 1875, the reservoir, then known as Montana Tract, was sold. Thomas J. Kelley and Dr. W. Lemoyne Wills bought the land for a business venture, but when the land boom busted, they men donated it to the city for a park.

During the recession of 1889 through 1891, the park was created. The first Superintendent of Parks was Joseph Tomlinson, an English immigrant who proposed and pioneered the park's design. It is said that he was homesick for Britain, especially his favorite park in Derbyshire, so he modeled Echo Park after the childhood playground.

At the same time, the reservoir was closed and the stream capped. It cost the city about $6,000 to do the work. The lake is no longer spring-fed but is filled with city water.

From where did the name Echo Park come? Again, it was a "gift" to Los Angeles from Tomlinson. One day while overseeing the construction, Tomlinson thought he heard his workers talking during a break, but he knew they were well across the park from him. He may have said, "This park has an echo!" One wonders how many times he yelled "hello" to test this theory. Regardless, the name stuck, and even though the landscaping that Tomlinson included destroyed the echo, the delightful story remains.

The origin of the famous bed of lotuses that grow in the lake, and are celebrated with the annual Lotus Festival, are a mystery. The urban myth says that evangelical missionaries planted them there for use as food, but no one knows the truth. The park, as movie buffs will tell you, was the "set" for many of the old Keystone Cops movies from Hollywood's early history.

If you should visit this Derbyshire-in-spirit park, be sure to look across the street at the Foursquare Gospel Church. It was built by evangelist Aimee Semple McPherson in the 1920s. A few blocks from the park you may want to visit the Victorian homes on Carroll Avenue to walk back into another time.

Echo Park is a replica of Derbyshire, England.
Courtesy of the USC Regional History Collection

The Modern School, featuring work such as that of Frank Lloyd Wright and Irving Gill, gave way to the Art Deco and Streamline Moderne. The Bullock's-Wilshire building in Los Angeles, designed by Englishman John Parkinson, is an example of the Art Deco style.

The Arroyo Culture took its name from *arroyo seco*, meaning "dry watercourse, creek, or riverbed." It refers to the bed that begins in the San Gabriel Mountains and flows past western Pasadena into the Los Angeles River. At the turn of the twentieth century, this area was the residence of choice for the rich and famous who were the outstanding and hopeful intellects, artists, writers, architects, and crafts people, including potters, weavers, furniture makers, tile makers, and book designers of the time.

These artists gathered in the area between 1890 and 1920, and their aesthetic lifestyle and creative approach gave expression to the ideas expressed by Englishman William Morris and furniture designer Gustav Stickley. The architectural mode embraced by this group was the Arts and Crafts, or Craftsman, style; but the English Tudor, Swiss Chalet, and Bavarian Hunting Lodge styles were also prized. Aspects of Hispanic and Indian cultures were influential, too.

The Eastlake style, named for English architect Charles Eastlake, is characterized by thin vertical shapes, jigsaw and lath work in wood, ornamental porch posts, and decorative knobs. Arcadia Railroad Station in Pomona is an example of the Eastlake style.

Art Deco architecture, all the rage in the early 1920s and still a part of our culture, features a heavy, formal look with ornamental zigzags, sunbursts, spirals, and stylized animals. It's known for glass bricks and flat roofs and can be seen in the El Rey Theater on Wilshire Miracle Mile.

CITY SKETCH

THE COLISEUM PARKINSON DESIGNED

The Los Angeles Memorial Coliseum was designed by English architect John Parkinson. Think again if you only connect the Coliseum with sports. Think, for a moment, how Parkinson would feel if he knew that his design resulted in the place where both John F. Kennedy and Pope John Paul II gave addresses.

The arena was completed in 1923 at a cost of just below $1 million and has twice hosted the Summer Olympics, in 1932 and 1984. Before Dodger Stadium was completed in Chavez Ravine, the Coliseum hosted the Los Angeles Dodgers, and it was the site of two Super Bowls (I and VI) and the World Series in 1959. The University of California, Los Angeles, played football at the Coliseum from 1933 to 1981.

Parkinson originally designed the arena to hold 75,000 people. City planners said attendance would never reach that limit. Yet, in 1932 it was expanded to hold 105,000 and it still wasn't enough. In the early 1990s it was refurbished in an attempt to keep the Los Angeles Raiders from leaving the city. The Raiders left anyway, but a far more severe blow was the 1994 Northridge earthquake, which damaged the structure.

The Los Angeles Memorial Coliseum is an official National Historic Landmark.

The Polo Field, Uplifters at
Rustic Canyon, January
the cars are parked facing North
Boulevard. The Polo Field is now G
Haverford Street and Rane

CHAPTER 6

Influence in Athletics

Even today in Southern California, most people are connected with active, outdoor lifestyles made possible by the temperate climate. For thousands of pioneers, homesteaders, and those who immigrated from the British Isles and Canada, the climate often was the reason for coming to the area.

Without modern medications, Southern California was the prescription for scores of ailments from tuberculosis to general malaise. Once in residence, newcomers, like those who preceded them, participated in the sports they loved "from back home" and those to which they would quickly become addicted. With the mild climate and large open spaces, athletics thrived, from tennis and polo to events we still see today in the Olympics.

Santa Monica Polo Grounds in the early 1900s.
Courtesy of the Santa Monica Historical Society

Polo Rules the Colony

Between matches at the Riverside Polo Club, afternoon tea was served and attended by Robert Lee Bettner, son of James, an English arrival at the colony of Riverside. Bettner was a key figure in polo in Southern California and in many of the social sporting events.

While historical accounts differ on the exact date that polo came to Southern California, it may have been introduced in 1878, when a group of riders with the United States Coastal Survey were stationed in Santa Monica and started a game with local Californios. The field's exact location is still under speculation. It may have been in Santa Monica at Ocean Avenue and Hotel Block, as many reports say, and then played in a canyon area on Sunset Boulevard. Suitable polo ponies were acquired at that time for about $50, a small fortune for the days.

The first polo club was established in 1892, according to English Colony writer and historian Tom Patterson in *Colony for California*. "The first field was on Jefferson Street near the railroad on land owned by the new English-owned Riverside Trust Company of which Matthew Gage was resident manager." Gage, an Irishman by birth, rarely played, although he was made president of the club and Bettner was secretary. Others who played were C. E. Maude, G. L. Waring, and William E. Pedley, all English-born residents of the colony. (Maude and Waring were also executives with the English-owned Riverside Trust Company, the citrus production company.)

Polo had originated in India, and when the British Army officers made it their game, the English image spread to other colonial groups. Since Riverside was determined to acquire that reflection, polo became the game of the upscale and socially conscious families of the area. As Patterson writes, "In the golden age of Queen Victoria, English manners and English social usage were held in the highest esteem among Americans with social ambitions." The polo grounds were established in 1896 at the intersection of Victoria Avenue and Van Buren Street, in Riverside.

Englishman and novelist Horace Annesley Vachell, author of novels such as *A Drama in Sunshine* and *The Procession of Life*, was an avid sportsman. He wrote in *Bunch Grass, a Chronicle of Life on a Cattle Ranch* (London, 1912), about the pleasures of the sporting life in the 1880s in California: "We worked and played, a happy combination although I must admit—not at all regretfully—that play came first in this sportsman's paradise, still a land of *manana*."

In the English colony in the San Gabriel and Riverside areas, Vachell believed, one must refuse to fall to the American habit of overwork. Ranchers and their families made time for sport, and historian Kevin Starr documents that Vachell was the one who introduced polo on his ranch in Southern California. Starr writes, "Upon the occasion of Queen Victoria's Golden Jubilee, [Vachell organized] a British-American match, the first official polo to be played west of the Rocky Mountains. Vachell, born into the life of country gentry, enjoyed polo, hunting, fishing, camping, and tennis, very much in keeping with the British colonial style and a way of relating to the non-English environment of Southern California while preserving one's feelings of caste.

Historian Kevin Starr writes (*Americans and the California Dream, 1850-1915*), "By 1897, *The Anglo-Californian*, the London-based journal of the English Colony in California, was reporting on matches held in Riverside which attracted crowds to the thousands." It was at this same period of our Southern California history that other British Isles sports, cricket and golf, became the thing to do amongst the upper classes.

Tennis Draws More Players

Most famous Britishers of Southern California tennis, without a doubt, were the Sutton sisters of Pasadena. And amongst her sisters, it was May Sutton Bundy who typically won honors and limelight on the courts. Tennis historians say, "What Babe Ruth was to baseball, May Sutton Bundy was to tennis."

English born, May Sutton Bundy was not only the first American of either sex to win at Wimbledon (1905 and 1907), but America's first female sports celebrity. She was the queen of the courts and the All England Tennis Club, and queen of the Pasadena Tournament of Roses.

May came from a tennis-playing family, the Suttons of Plymouth, England, and then of Pasadena, where they owned a ten-acre citrus grove at Mountain Street and Hill Avenue. May, Violet, Florence and Ethel ruled the world of tennis. The family legacy continued with stars

"As I remember the strokes in those days, the forehand drive was the prevalent weapon possessed by most women, all their other strokes suffering by comparison. If I had any advantage over the girls in the East playing at the time it was the fact that I could volley and smash overhead. I loved the net position and had had perfect training in a safe method of approach, for all the young years of my tennis career I played against that severe tyrant, May Sutton, who possessed a terrific forehand passing shot. My only hope against her was to get a return deep into her backhand court and then to come to the net, for her backhand was defensive."

—MARY K. BROWNE, "NET PLAY CONTINUES TO WIN,"
SOUTHERN CALIFORNIA TENNIS CHAMPIONS CENTENNIAL, 1987.

including Dorothy "Dodo" Bundy Cheney, who won 298 tournament tiles, and grandson Brian Cheney, the nation's third-ranked singles player and part of the No. 1 doubles combination in the 1940s. The Sutton's great-grandchildren are still very active in the game.

English immigrant and Altadena resident Arthur Allen, who at 18 won the singles championship of the first tennis club in Southern California, the San Gabriel Lawn Tennis Club, encouraged his progeny to play the game, too. Allen's father, William, was the owner of the Sphinx Ranch, so called because Allen (born in the north of England) had a thriving cotton business in Egypt for 23 years before returning to Bath, England, and then immigrating to Southern California.

Historians, including Richard D. Sears, in *Southern California Tennis Champions Centennial*, explain that the Allens were very

British and were keen on tennis. They brought the first tennis racquets to Southern California and were the first to have their own courts.

Sears writes, "They went every Wednesday afternoon to the George Stoneman place in Alhambra to play tennis, and after Stoneman became governor of the state, they went to the Purcell place in San Gabriel…much pent-up energy was worked off with racquets. There were always assembly dances and the family attended public and private parties all over the valley. And with such a large family, there was always something doing. And that was the Altadena of long ago."

Historically Speaking

"Tennis success of present day Southern California net stars is, in large measure, directly traceable to William H. Young. Canadian born, he went to Oxford University early in the 1870s where he was among those who took up the new game of lawn tennis.

"After graduation, he returned to Canada, but instead of pursuing a career in his native country, moved to Southern California. Arriving in Santa Monica in the summer of 1879, he met some members of the Allen family of Altadena, who spent their summer months at the seashore. To his surprise, Mr. Young found the Allens had a tennis kit. Quickly a crude net was set up on one of the streets of Santa Monica, near where the Municipal Pier now stands, and in the dust was played, as far as is known, the first game in Southern California."

—H. ARCHIE RICHARDSON, "CALIFORNIA TENNIS DATES BACK TO 1870s,"
THE CHRISTIAN SCIENCE MONITOR, APRIL 28, 1948.

MAY SUTTON BUNDY ENGRAVED HER SKILL IN TENNIS

Called the Queen of Tennis, May Sutton Bundy (1888-1975) defied Victorian mores, rolled up her sleeves, and trampled her tennis opponents. While the years may make the old photos of May seem quaint, she was a terror and trendsetter on the courts throughout Southern California and England.

May, her siblings, and parents arrived in Southern California from Plymouth, England in 1893. According to family stories, Adolphus DeGruchy Sutton, the tennis star's father, named his daughter because she was large, a 16-pound baby. Toasting the birth, Sutton, a yachting enthusiast, is said to have remarked, "She has a beam about as broad as May [his favorite schooner]. Think we'll name her May."

While the Suttons settled into Southern California life and mingled with others from the British Isles, tennis was always close to their hearts, especially for May. By the time there were seven Sutton children, they were enlisting the help of English neighbors to haul mud from a nearby canyon to press into a clay tennis court.

May Sutton Bundy was the youngest female Wimbledon champion until Tracey Austin.
Courtesy of the Santa Monica Historical Society

At 12, Sutton won her first open tournament, defeating her older sister, Ethel. The next year, she won the first of many titles in the Pacific Southwest tournament, beating a 22-year old woman. In 1904, she won the U.S. title, becoming the nation's youngest woman champion. She held this title for almost eight decades, until Tracy Austin, at 16 years and 9 months, snatched it away.

At 18, she rolled up her sleeves, shocked British society, and won a singles title at Wimbledon, defeating England's Kate Douglas Chambers. Reports say that the crowd stared in disbelief as the upstart Sutton threw her arms in the air in victory. It's said that the soon-to-be King George V was sitting in his royal box weeping.

London newspaper headlines shouted: Pasadena Washer Woman Wins. Reports said: "May Sutton looks like she's taking in washing." All, except Sutton and her entourage and cheering section, were appalled with the impropriety of rolling up one's sleeves *in public*. Sutton smiled through the entire event, never losing her sense of humor or determination. Reports say she was treated like a truck driver at a royal garden party. Her unrestrained enthusiasm and athletic expertise continued as she returned to Wimbledon two years later and snatched another victory.

When Sutton reigned on another court, the court of the 1908 Tournament of Roses, she rolled her sleeves down, donned a frilly dress and twirled a pink umbrella. She was queen and her sister Florence was a princess. May rode again in the Tournament of Roses parade in 1975 on the float sponsored by the city of Santa Monica, the city where one of the first tennis matches was played.

In 1912, May married Thomas Clark Bundy, a onetime national doubles champion, who would later win twice more before entering business. While business was Bundy's career, his wife juggled motherhood and tennis. In 1915, a few months after giving birth to their second child, Sutton Bundy returned to the court, eventually winning the Southern California title.

In 1920, Bundy bought 5½ acres near Melrose Avenue and Vine Street and built the Los Angeles Tennis Club. Here May Sutton Bundy played serious exhibition games against such stars as Marlene Dietrich, Jean Harlow, Joan Bennett, Charlie Chaplin, and Clark Gable, along with Wimbledon tennis champs like Helen Wills and Helen Jacobs.

May Sutton Bundy's tennis stardom is impossible to match and her determination to excel and be well educated was mirrored in her family. All the Sutton sisters continued their tennis stardom at college and many continued to play after receiving their degrees.

Just a few months before her death in 1975, Sutton Bundy played another match and won. Her legacy includes being named at 42 one of nation's most influential women, the first woman to be inducted into the U.S. Lawn Tennis Association's Hall of Fame, and scores of personal and public triumphs over sexism and age discrimination. May Sutton Bundy played the games of tennis and life to win.

"Golf…is the infallible test. The man who can go into a patch of rough alone, with the knowledge that only God is watching him, and play his ball where it lies, is the man who will serve you faithfully and well."

—P. G. WODEHOUSE, *THE CLICKING OF CUTHBERT* (1922)

On the Links

Those from the British Isles and Canada also made time for golf. In the English Colony in Riverside, for example, links already existed and had to be moved when more citrus groves were needed, circa 1880. The Polo and Golf Club of Riverside participated in its first statewide golf tournament with C. E. Maude, English-born citrus executive, winning the state championship in 1899. Also in 1899 the Southern California Golf Association was established, and Maud became its first president. Golf was a primary social activity for those in the English enclaves and among immigrants from the British Isles and Canada.

Toss the Puck

Ice hockey is a game whereby two opposing teams attempt to drive the puck (a hard round, flat-sided object) through the goal of the opponent by means of sticks that are curved or hooked on one end. Historians say that hockey may be the oldest of all ball-and-stick games, known to ancient Egyptians, Greeks, Persians, Romans, and Arabs. The name "hockey" may have been adopted by the English, from the French hoquet, or shepherd's crook, a name used in the eighteenth century. The name wasn't universally adopted until the nineteenth century, though.

Ice hockey was probably a descendant of bandy, a sport developed in England in the late eighteenth century and revised either in 1853 or 1860 by British soldiers stationed in Canada. Students at McGill University in Montreal set up the rules in 1879 and they've been modified a number of times for current (and safer play). The first game in the United States is believed to have been played in 1893.

Wayne Gretzky (b. 1961) is considered to be the greatest of all ice hockey players. Born in Brantford, Ontario, Canada, Gretzky came

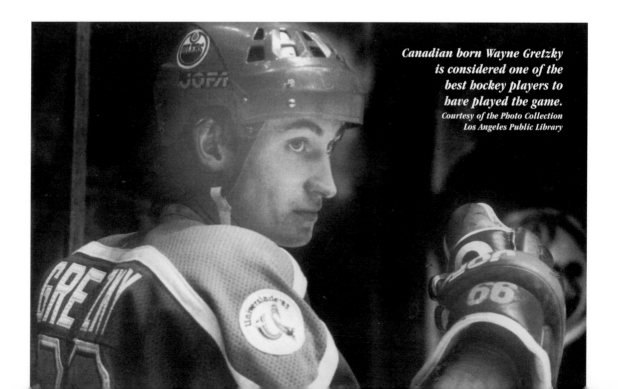

Canadian born Wayne Gretzky is considered one of the best hockey players to have played the game.
Courtesy of the Photo Collection
Los Angeles Public Library

"Now I know why 300,000 Canadians moved here. To get *away* from hockey."

—Sports promoter and onetime owner of the Los Angeles Kings, Jack Kent Cooke, c. 1967.

to Los Angeles to play with the Los Angeles Kings in 1988 after leading the Edmonton Oilers to four Stanley Cup victories (in 1983-84, 1984-85, 1986-87, and 1987-88). Gretzky won the Art Ross Memorial Trophy for the National Hockey League's highest scorer for seven consecutive years, from the 1980-81 season to the 1986-87 season.

In the 1989-90 season, Gretzky broke long-time hockey legend Gordie Howe's NHL all-time record for number of goals in regular season play (894). While Gretzky has played with other teams, including the St. Louis Blues, the New York Rangers, and the Anaheim Mighty Ducks, Gretzky's best remembered for his seasons with the Kings. After nearly two decades, Gretzky still holds most of the league's major scoring records and more NHL records than any other player. "The Great One," as he was dubbed, retired from professional play after the 1998-99 season and was inducted into the Hockey Hall of Fame in 1999. His career totals include 2,857 points and 894 goals. The NHL retired his jersey number (99) after his final game. Today, Gretzky gives time and shares his good fortune with various charities throughout Southern California.

CHAPTER 7

Influence in Commerce

Initially, California was thought suitable to support only cattle and sheep ranches. Gradually, long-forgotten pioneers established early commercial enterprises, conducting business in and out of Southern California. Then the early Mexican ranchos, along with some of the missions, planted crops such as olives and some oranges. But with the arrival of working ranchers including William Wolfskill, Don Juan Forster, Hugo Reid, James Irvine, Matthew Gage, and others, commerce in Southern California burst wide open.

Santa Monica was founded by Welshman John P. Jones and was a hub of culture and commerce.
Courtesy of the USC Regional History Collection

119

"*I* am afraid I have no aptitude for commerce. I didn't even enjoy being ship's super-cargo on the voyage out, except that it kept me off the yardarms and away from the bilge pumps rounding the Horn."

—NICHOLAS DEN, C. 1834, SOON TO BECOME THE OWNER OF THE LARGEST AND RICHEST RANCHO IN THE SANTA BARBARA AREA, DOS PUEBLOS, NATIVE OF GARANDARA, COUNTY KILKENNY, IRELAND.

Portrait

ARTHUR VEITCH 1850 –1926

*T*oday, the name of Arthur Veitch, born in Woodstock, Ontario, Canada, might not be familiar. But in Los Angeles during the early 1900s, he saved countless lives and helped ease suffering with the supplies of medical equipment he had available in his downtown Los Angeles store.

His father and many other family members were physicians and surgeons, and young Arthur, while interested in the field, wanted to strike out on his own. For the sake of his health as it was with others who immigrated to Southern California, Veitch opened a medical supply emporium with the finest drugs and surgical instruments the country knew. The supplies were sold up and down the coast of California.

While World War I signaled the end of his business, since it was impossible to fulfill medical orders since the supplies were sent to the war front, Veitch turned his attention to patriotic causes and church work, active in the Episcopal Church at Los Angeles.

A PLACE CALLED WILLMORE CITY

*I*n the 1870s Englishman William Erwin Willmore, came to Southern California, not for gold but to start subdividing and developing a city. He landed by ship in the port of Wilmington and walked to Anaheim by the route that is now Anaheim Street in Long Beach. Urban myth says that Willmore stopped in Long Beach and gazed down at the grassy plain that bordered the beach and dreamed of a "long beach" and a new colony.

In the 1880s, he bought an option on land from the Bixby brothers, colleagues of James Irvine, and purchased 4,000 acres to organize his "American Colony." Water was not a problem in the area, as it seemed to be in other communities, since there were abundant artesian wells, many still flourishing today. His hope was to sell parcels of 5 to 40 acres for nuts, citrus, cattle, and tropical fruit farming. He began advertising in the Midwestern newspapers about the fertile land, year-round sunshine, and abundant (read that cheap) land. They came by train—by the hundreds. Willmore drew up grandiose resolutions, but with the financial panic of the 1850 and then the land bust, he ran out of money and patience. The scheme was abandoned.

The Oranges Rolled Out

When the oranges started rolling out, suddenly California became known for agriculture, and even in today's high-tech science- and computer-oriented world, California is the home to the largest agricultural economy and its associated commerce in the nation. If you're eating fruits, nuts, or vegetables anywhere out of the state, there's a 50-50 chance that it was produced or processed in California. That's because California produces 55 percent of the nations nuts, fruits, and produce.

According to the California Department of Agriculture, the state's agriculture is more than just food. Farmers contribute to the creation of products related to manufacturing, health care, printing, education, recreation, transportation, entertainment, construction, and personal care. That means everything from detergents, x-ray film, paper, shampoo, toothpaste, footballs, shoes, flowers, tires, antifreeze, and baseball bats. From the ports in San Diego to the fields in the Coachella Valley, this area is one of the world's largest "supermarkets."

Since the 1950s California has been the number one agricultural state in the nation, and more than $70 billion is generated annually

Orange Grove in Redlands. Commerce and agriculture merged to establish Southern California as the fruit basket of the world.
Courtesy of the USC Regional History Collection

by this industry. In Southern California dollars, that means San Diego county leads the country in indoor decorative and nursery crops ($957 billion), Riverside County stars with milk and grapes ($1.142 trillion), and Imperial County is the largest producer of alfalfa and cattle ($957 billion). These figures reflect the 1996 valuation.

With agriculture as the seed, commerce has taken over and includes everything from oil to tourism.

Portrait

SENATOR JOHN P. JONES
Founder of Santa Monica, 1829 –1912

Born in Wales, raised in Ohio, with time in the mines of Virginia City and as a senator from Nevada, John P. Jones is most often remembered as the founder of Santa Monica. Although he had little formal education, Jones became a distinguished orator. It is said that he had the ability of making columns of figures sound as fascinating as a novel. He was an avid student of humanity and books, a patron of arts and letters, and one of the most respected and wealthiest men of his time. The home he built, Miramar, was equipped with only the finest, including a popular tennis court for friends including the Sutton sisters and members of the Allen family of Altadena.

Caring more for people than what money could buy, he and his wife, Georgina Sullivan Jones, gave generously to parks, including land that is now Santa Monica. Today a stone bench and monument stands in recognition for John P. Jones work and life. It can be visited at Palisades Park in Los Angeles and holds a special meaning since the coastline it graces was one of Jones favorite places. The inscription says, "In the evening of his life, John P. Jones used to come each day to watch the sun set over the ocean."

"The Commissioner of Internal Revenue has decided that dressmaking is a manufacturer, and as such, if carried on to an extent exceeding $1,000 per year, including price of goods, requires a license. The dressmaker is required to make monthly returns, and to pay a tax of three cent on the whole value of her manufactures."

—Frank Leslie's *Illustrated Newspaper*, January 10, 1863.

Oil: Southern California's Propellant

The oil fields of Southern California were well known to the Native Americans. The Gabrieleno Indians used the sticky, tarry substance to waterproof baskets. Later, settlers would use the tar to protect the roofs of their adobe homes.

Visitors to the interpretive center at the La Brea Tar Pits in downtown Los Angeles can learn the story of how prehistoric animals were lured to their death into pits in which great, water-like substances oozed from the ground. In 1769, Captain de Portola's men documented the seepage. Early Spanish, English, and American ranchers kept cattle away from the pits, where they could fall in and die. Pio Pico and the missionary fathers collected the tar, distilled it, and used the oil for lamps at the San Fernando mission.

For modern purposes, the first oil was "discovered" at Pico Canyon, in the San Fernando Valley, about 1850. In 1859, on property near Los Angeles belonging to Maj. Henry Hancock, a whale oil salesman (whose name has been lost in time) set up a still and produced semi-liquid asphaltum before Hancock ran him off the property. In 1865 The Pioneer Oil Company drilled for oil near Newhall. The board of directors included Irishman and former governor John Gately Downey, along with Phineas Banning, Benjamin Davis Wilson, and Winfield S. Hancock. In the mid-1870s, the company became Star Oil, which changed its name to Pacific Coast Oil and would eventually become Standard Oil.

In the drilling frenzy that pulsated through Southern California in the 1880s, wells sprang up even in the best neighborhoods. Historians say that Signal Hill, now known for refineries, was once proposed as an upscale residential area, until oil was discovered.

The first well drilled within the city of Los Angeles was at the corner of 2nd Street and Glendale Boulevard. By 1897 the city had more than 500 derricks dotting the town. The once-lovely suburbs of Santa Monica Boulevard and Vermont Avenue had become a shantytown for immigrant workers.

Historians point out that drilling reached new heights in the 1920s when finds were made in Whittier, Montebello, Compton, Torrance, and Inglewood. Upton Sinclair captured the scenes of oil madness and the after effects of the mayhem in his 1926 novel *Oil!*

"Oil!" was the cry throughout much of Southern California. It seemed that oil was everywhere from Santa Barbara to Orange County, including beneath the ocean floor. From 1953 to 1988, some 1,000 wells pumped 375 million barrels of oil from the Los Angeles area alone. With the discovery of vast offshore deposits, it seemed in the 1960s that drilling rigs would clutter the entire Southern California coastline. Environmentally aware and much-outraged citizens fought back, although rigs now are a permanent sight in Santa Barbara and other spots on the coast. But many drillers abandoned their offshore drilling plans and those wells that are on land are now better camouflaged than they were in the past.

And by Air

The aircraft industry was established well before World War I and later produced an economy that still affects Southern California. It may have all begun in the area that is now called Otay Mesa, in San Diego. John Joseph Montgomery, whose mother came from Ireland and whose father arrived in San Diego from England, supposedly piloted the first glider flight.

Urban myths often mix with reality, and there's much confusion as to whether Montgomery actually achieved the first controlled flight, launched in a glider off a San Diego hillside on August 28, 1883. If he did, then this descendant from the British Isles shouldn't be forgotten in our history. According to a longtime resident of the San Diego community of San Ysidro (*Union Tribune, "Monument to Flight, or Fancy?"* April 3, 2000 pp. 1 and 3), Joyce Hettich, 93, said she once met a man who claimed to have witnessed the historic flight.

"He was going rabbit hunting one morning and saw a wagon pull up with two men and a girl. He (Hettich cannot recall his name) saw them fly. The man confided that he finally stopped telling people because no one believed him," Hettich said. "When James (John Montgomery's twin brother and assistant) was here, he took me to the seventh olive tree and said, 'This is where I was when it went over my head.'" Montgomery's conquest of glider flight has never been totally authenticated. Some people insist this achievement belonged to Waldo Waterman, who in 1909 glided from a hill where San Diego's Balboa Park is now. Yet, it is documented that by 1905, Montgomery's gliders were so famous that they were being dropped by hot-air balloons over carnivals. Fairgoers watched in awe as the aircraft silently gilded to the ground. Montgomery earned a doctorate from what is now Santa Clara University, where substantial amounts of his developmental work is kept. He taught mathematics at Saint Joseph College in Rohnerville, built an experimental wind tunnel, and invented an early electric typewriter.

In 1911 Montgomery experimented with a new glider design, and crashed to his death. While Waterman is immortalized in the International Aerospace Hall of Fame in Balboa Park, Montgomery is not. But there is an airfield in San Diego that bears his name.

A ROYAL RANCHO IN SANTA BARBARA

Nicholas Den, from County Kilkenny, Ireland, had hoped to become a doctor. In 1834, when financial reversals came upon his family, he left Trinity College in Dublin and headed to America in order to seek his fortune. The East Coast was but a stopping point, and he fell in love with California at first sight. Over time, Den would acquire the largest rancho in the Santa Barbara area, a royal rancho, indeed. After his death, the land was divided amongst his ten children, and each envisioned his or her own way to make the land successful.

At one time the ranch was a showplace for thoroughbred horses, then it was to become a spa of world-renowned notoriety. That was realized only on paper, though. Kate Den Bell, daughter of Den, fought the courts and won back the ranch. Many believe that she somehow knew that the property was rich in oil.

This same rancho will go down in history as the only land to be shelled by Japanese submarines in 1942. In the 1960s it become known for orchids, carnations, birds-of-paradise, and Easter lilies that were shipped around the world.

As historian Walker A. Tompkins writes, "Perhaps one Dos Pueblos pilgrim in a thousand has heard the name of Nicholas A. Den, the pioneer who has slept for nearly a century in his tomb at Santa Barbara Mission; the runaway lad from Erin who, arriving almost penniless in pastoral California, was able to build a ranch kingdom out of hides and tallow and adobe and horseflesh." Perhaps now that has changed.

Nicholas Den was one of the earliest Irishmen to own land in Santa Barbara.
Courtesy of the Photo Collection/Los Angeles Public Library

128

H. J. WHITLEY,
the "Father" of Hollywood

Hobart "H. J." Johnstone Whitley (1860-1931) was a Toronto, Canada-born land developer of English and Scottish descent. He took the ideas of nineteenth-century French social philosopher Charles Fourier and began to create towns for the Great Northern Railroad. In 1909 he was part of the Los Angeles Suburban Homes Company that bought up and developed the San Fernando Valley. In his charge, the syndicate purchased 47,500 acres from the Lankershim-Van Nuys family and began building more towns.

The syndicate and Whitley were implicated in the scandal of William Mulholland's Owens Valley water project, where public water was brought into the San Fernando Valley through unfair practices. Whitley was one of the largest landholders.

In addition to helping establish the towns of Reseda, Sherman Oaks, Tarzana, and Woodland Hills, in the 1920s H. J. developed an upscale neighborhood in Hollywood called Whitley Heights. One of the streets in Sherman Oaks was named Sutton, after Altadena's star tennis player May Sutton and the founding family.

Mrs. Margaret Virginia Ross Whitley was the first to start a kindergarten in Hollywood, building a room onto their spacious home and paying the teachers.

Because of the effort and energy of Whitley in the land development of Southern California, he was dubbed the "Father of Hollywood."

Bullock's Department Store was founded by Canadian John G. Bullock.
Courtesy of the Photo Department/Los Angeles Public Library

 s Southern California grew in what seems like non-stop momentum, immigrants from the British Isles and Canada continued to form commerce. Bullock's Department stores, a major mercantile chain known throughout Southern California, was founded in 1907 by Canadian John G. Bullock. Another Englishman Arthur Letts, founded

Broadway Department Stores (later to be sold to R. H. Macy & Co.), one of the largest mercantile houses in the West.

The first Bullock's was located in downtown Los Angeles. The second store, more upscale this time and also designed by Englishman John Parkinson, was Bullock's Wilshire. It is now the Southwestern University School of Law.

The store was opened in 1929 on a bean field near Vermont Avenue. Historians Leonard Pitt and Dale Pitt, in *Los Angeles A to Z,* write, "This [was] the first suburban department store in the nation. An estimated 30,000 people jammed the building on its opening day."

Eventually, the department store would become part of the Arthur Letts enterprises and would be known as I. Magnin/Bullock's Wilshire. The building is in the Art Deco architectural style.

Historically Speaking

"You can see those graves, with a picket fence about them, and no derrick for a hundred feet or more. Someday all those unlovely derricks will be gone, and so will the picket fence and the graves. [Oil] is an evil Power which roams the earth, crippling the bodies of men and women, and luring the nations to destruction by visions of unearned wealth, and the opportunity to enslave and exploit labor."

—Upton Sinclair, *Oil*, 1926.

Portrait

PHILANTHROPIST AND SHOPKEEPER ARTHUR LETTS

Through his life, Arthur Letts (1862-1923) would be called a scholar, English entrepreneur, shopkeeper, and visionary. He was also a man who cared for humanity, especially children, and spent nine years as president of the Los Angeles Y.M.C.A. He was also active with the Boy Scouts of America. Letts was one of the first employers to offer a mutual benefit association, providing relief to employees kept from their jobs because of illness, unheard of in the early part of the twentieth century.

Born at Holmby Lodge, in Northamptonshire, England, his birthplace was an estate that had been in the family for over four hundred years. In Hollywood he built a mansion called Holmby House. It was on this property that Letts would allow his zeal for gardening and horticulture to surface. His collection of cacti and succulents was once considered the largest and finest in the world. The federal government recognized his garden as a United States substation for plant propagation. In 1912, he was selected to represent America on the advisory board for the International Horticultural Exhibition in London.

In 1896, Letts opened his first Broadway store on 4th and Broadway in Los Angeles, which was practically out in the country then. It was so popular that in 1903 about 30,000 visited the store in a single evening. At this time there were only about 130,000 residents in Los Angeles.

Arthur Letts founded the Broadway Department Store, which is now Macy's.
Courtesy of the Photo Collection/Los Angeles Public Library

In 1915, Letts opened his flagship, nine-story store in what is now downtown Los Angeles. It had 14 passenger elevators and was patronized by 60,000 on opening day. It featured a nursery, hospital, writing rooms, restaurants, and a "silence room," where women suffering exhaustion or strained nerves from shopping could retire for absolute silence and complete rest.

In addition to the commerce of a department store chain, Letts was involved in a string of successful enterprises throughout Southern California. He was at one time vice president of the California Savings Bank and director of the Broadway Bank and Trust. He handled large real estate deals, and in 1919 purchased the Wolfskill ranch of over 3,000 acres.

Tourism has always played a large role in Southern California. The actual term "tourism" may have originated in Southern California, suggest historians, because after the transcontinental railroad linked the United States, tour groups were formed to visit the West. Railroads promoted art shows and produced magazines, such as *Sunset*, which is still going strong after more than 100 years. Tourist attractions like Disneyland, Hollywood, and the *Queen Mary* attract millions of visitors each year.

Tourism, at one time, however, was for the birds. Ostrich farms, once thought to be the "crop" of the future, were introduced into Southern California from the British colonial possession of South Africa. In 1910 there were about 10 large farms. The Cawston Ostrich Farm, in South Pasadena, was owned by Edwin Cawston, originally from Cobham, England. It was located on Henry E. Huntington's Red Line, the Pacific Electric Railway line that connected downtown Los

Angeles to the suburbs. The farms were a major tourist attraction and a successful commercial enterprise.

Leonard Pitt and Dale Pitt, in *Los Angeles A to Z*, write, "At one time hundreds, perhaps thousands, of birds were raised there. An 1897 magazine advertisement promised children rides on the backs of the birds, while ladies were lured by quality ornamental feathers that could be fashioned into boas, capes, and collars." In the 1930s, Cawston's claimed to be the oldest ostrich farm in the nation.

Portrait

EMMELINE FRANCES BANKS, M.D.
Medicine for Babies

𝒟r. Banks was known during the 1920s and 1930s as the city of Pasadena's "baby doctor." She stood as a role model for young women hoping to branch out from the stereotypical future of being a wife and mother. Dr. Banks, born in Essex, England, came to the United States as a teenager, became a teacher in Oregon, and then worked for two years in the Baptist Missionary Training School in Chicago.

Her ambition to become a doctor continued to surface and she re-focused her work with two years in medical courses at McMinnville College and the University of Oregon, where she received her medical degree.

Dr. Banks taught pediatrics and pathology at Women's Medical College and Hospital in Philadelphia when few women worked in medicine. She came to Pasadena in 1927, where she set up a practice that specialized in helping women and children.

BRITISH AMERICAN CHAMBER OF COMMERCE

The British American Chamber of Commerce provides the opportunity for business people to meet professionally, socially, and culturally as well as develop business contacts and friendships with American and British interests. It acts as a point of liaison between the British Consulate General, other chambers of commerce, and commercial institutions on matters relating to conducts of trade, It encourages trade between the United Kingdom and the United States.

The Chamber and its co-sponsors support more than 10,000 corporations as part of the British American Business Council, as well as related organizations such as the Los Angeles World Trade Center Association, the Los Angeles Junior Chamber of Commerce, and the Council of European-American Chambers. The Chamber also publishes a quarterly newsletter, *Britannicus*, that communicates the programs and activities of the organization. The Chamber offers assistance in dealing with all aspects of British/American relations, maintains a business law library, and travel assistance.

Patron Sponsors

Align-Rite International
Arthur Andersen LLP
British Airways
Comms People Inc.

J & H Marsh McLennan, Inc.
KPMG Peat Marwick LLP
Pricewaterhouse Coopers LLP
Sunkist Growers

Premier Sponsors

Aggie Hoffman, Immigration Law
Air New Zealand
American Airlines
Aqua 4 Corporation
AON Risk Services, Inc.
Arter & Hadden LLP
Asherson & Klein Immigration Law
British Whole Sale Imports Inc.
Cable & Wireles, Inc.

Capital Relations Inc.
City National Bank
Computec International Resources, Inc.
Continental Airlines
Deloitte & Touche LLP
Ernst & Young
Galpin Jaguars
Harvey Titanium Ltd.

Jaguar Cars Inc.
Joseph Cohen Computing
Princess Cruises
Ronlo Engineering
Tiffany & Co.
The Joseph Scott Company
Virgin Atlantic Airways
Ye Old Kings Head

RNAMENT OF ROSES NEW YEARS DAY.

1906 Tournament of Roses Parade in Pasadena, home to many British residents.
Courtesy of the Pasadena Historical Museum

CHAPTER 8

Influence in the Arts and Entertainment

From Welsh bards and no-nonsense newspaper reporters to the glamour worlds of movie stars and entertainers, Southern California attracted a profuse array of creativity from the British Isles and Canada. It still does.

Southern California was more than sunshine and oranges after the Civil War, through the land booms, and into the new century. It was brimming with those whose voices would be heard and those who wanted to stop the noise. When the movie industry came to the area in the early 1900s, would-be superstars and anyone who needed a job flocked to the area. The personality of Los Angeles, for instance, was in for a change.

Once thought to be populated only by those of the highest moral regard, "those movie people," as the film stars became known, provided titillating conversations in parlors and churches and at highbrow afternoon teas where gossip and scandal were often on the menu.

The arts community, including the Arroyo Culture mentioned in the chapter on architecture, held fast to the Victorian beliefs that everything was proper and above board, at least on the surface.

As Southern California became a mecca for the rich and powerful, those fleeing the winters of the East and Midwest demanded that culture be available.

In the 1870s and 1880s the theater often depended on traveling troupes for readings and minstrel shows. In 1884 Ozro Childs Grand Opera House was built on Main Street, near 1st, in Los Angeles. The inaugural performance was the eighteenth century English comedy *School for Scandal*, by Richard Brinsley Sheridan. By 1887 a visiting Shakespearean troupe was netting as much as $17,936 in one week.

The Los Angeles Theater on Spring Street, built in 1888, hosted Maurice Barrymore, Lillian Russell, and Sarah Bernhardt. England's most famous actress of the time, Mrs. Patrick Campbell, performed in Los Angeles, bringing Henrick Ibsen's *Rosmersholdm* to the Belasco Theatre in 1908.

Live theater had a hard time surviving in the early part of the twentieth century, yet after World War I there was a revival. The Hollywood Bowl was constructed in the 1920s, and the Ramona Pageant (based on the life of the Scotch Paisano Hugo Reid and his Native American wife) began in Hemet in 1923 and still plays there today.

BEAUTY AND BRAINS

Mary Pickford (1893-1979) was not only a beautiful silent screen actress, but she also knew the business side of Hollywood. Born in Toronto, Canada, she began acting at age 5. At 16, she arrived in Los Angeles, and filmmaker D. W. Griffith hired her on at the Biograph Studio. The studio was really a renovated lumberyard at the corner of Grand Avenue and Washington Street. Pickford would star in scores of films and earned the title of "America's Sweetheart," which came with a price tag of $1,000 a week as she played adorable, funny young girls.

When married to actor Douglas Fairbanks, they owned Pickfair, a Beverly Hills mansion designed as a hunting lodge, located on the highest point of the city, and built for about $35,000. It became a gathering place for Hollywood celebrities. In recent years Pickford's home has been reconstructed from near total demolition at a cost in excess of $11 million. Pickford and Fairbanks also bought property in San Diego County. They would retreat to this wild land of quiet and sagebrush, camp among the chaparral, and plan their new home. While the couple divorced before the building started, San Diego still remembers them, and the upscale suburb of Fairbanks Ranch is now populated by elite families that would make Pickford and Fairbanks feel quite comfortable.

Actress Mary Pickford was known as America's sweetheart.
**Courtesy of the Photo Collection
Los Angeles Public Library**

Pickford became one of the highest paid and most powerful women in Hollywood and, one might say, in all of North America. With Fairbanks, Griffith, and Charlie Chaplin, Pickford was the founder and principal stockholder in United Artists. Historians and movie trivia buffs point out that Pickford's brother and sister, Jack and Lottie, were also in her movies.

Film buffs will remember her in *Her First Biscuits* (1909) and *Ramona* (1910). Lesser-known roles were in *The Little American*, about the sinking of the Lusitania, where according to biographers, Pickford had to endure the frigid water off San Pedro harbor dressed in an evening gown. In 1933, Pickford was the first female grand marshal of the Tournament of Roses Parade.

CITY SKETCH

HOLLYWOOD
Glamour That Started in Hay

Long before the Native American land was known as Rancho La Brea or Rancho Los Feliz, the area was a desired hunting ground. By 1870 a strong agricultural and farming community flourished in what we now call Hollywood. On a clear, balmy spring day, it's obvious why hay and grain, bananas and pineapples thrived in the semi-tropical area.

When the ranchos were subdivided during the land boom years, H. H. Wilcox purchased an area for a large villa. *The Los Angeles Express* newspaper (May 15, 1887) printed a story saying that Wilcox planned the drive in front of the villa to be "the finest drive in Los Angeles County, being 100 feet wide and five miles long." Mrs. Daeida Wilcox christened the community alongside their drive Hollywood. Wilcox was aggressive, and within a few years the area was a planned community with paved streets. Prospect Avenue, now Hollywood Boulevard, was the center of the plan, and large residential lots were sold to wealthy men and women from the East and Midwest so they could "winter in California."

1930 Los Angeles, between Broadway and 3rd.
Courtesy of the Photo Collection/Los Angeles Public Library

Soon, mansions in the Queen Anne, Victorian, and Mission Revival styles populated Hollywood. Churches and schools sprang forth from the area, and in 1903 it was incorporated. But the lack of water forced annexation to the city of Los Angeles in 1910. In 1911 the Nestor Company opened Hollywood's first film studio in an old tavern on Sunset and Gower. Cecil B. DeMille and D. W. Griffith began making movies in Hollywood and throughout Los Angeles because of the long, dry months, clear outdoor lighting, and moderate climate.

In the 1930s high-rise office buildings sprang to life, and homes were destroyed to make way for commerce. Clubs, movie houses, and restaurants mushroomed on every street, changing the elegant grandeur of the area to storefronts and bustling traffic jams. The city has since seen even more changes, yet Hollywood Boulevard is officially listed in the National Register of Historic Places, which protects the significance of Hollywood's past.

Portrait

BOB HOPE
Comedian/Actor/Extraordinary Human

When told he'd just received an honorary knighthood from Queen Elizabeth in 1998, Bob Hope quipped, "What an honor and what a surprise for a boy born in England, raised in Cleveland and schooled in vaudeville." That's Bob Hope and an extraordinary man for all times.

Born May 29, 1903 in Eltham, England, Hope immigrated with his parents to the United States in 1907. After years on the stage as a dancer and comedian, he made his first film appearance in *The Big Broadcast of 1938* and sang what would become his song, "Thanks for the Memory." In his partnership with Bing Crosby and Dorothy Lamour, he appeared in the highly successful and timeless *Road to…* movies between 1940 and 1952, and in scores of others.

Beginning in World War II and continuing through cold wars, the Korean War and the conflict in Vietnam, Hope pledged his untiring energies and financial reserves to entertain the troops stationed throughout

Bob Hope, America's beloved comedian, created an enduring legacy for his endless commitment to entertaining the U.S. troops overseas.
Courtesy of the USC Regional History Collection

the world. For these actions and his contributions to the entertainment industry, above and beyond the call of duty as a fine actor and comedian, Hope was given a special Academy Award on five different occasions. The 1959 Emmy Award given to Hope summed up the thoughts of many: Thank you, Bob Hope, "for bringing the great gift of laughter to all peoples of all nations; for selflessly entertaining American troops throughout the world over many years; and for making TV finer by these deeds and by the consistently high quality of your TV programs throughout the years."

Other awards include the 1994 American Comedy Award for Lifetime Achievement, the 1985 Kennedy Center Honors Lifetime Achievement Award, the 1965 Screen Actors Guild Life Achievement Ward, the 1962 Hollywood Foreign Press Association Cecil B. DeMille Award, and scores of others.

Currently living in Rancho Mirage, near Palm Springs, California, Hope and his wife, Dolores, have four adopted children. Ever the jokester and always a golfer at heart, Hope recently quipped, "Golf is my real profession. Show business pays my greens fees."

Historically Speaking

"California has the climate of the lands which have given the world its noblest religions, its soundest philosophy, its highest art, its greatest poets and painters and sculptors and musicians. There does not seem to be anything bad for the intellect or the heart in the sort of climate that has mothered Jesus of Nazareth, and Homer and Socrates, and Praxiteles, Plato, Virgil, Michelangelo, Titian, Correggio, Velasquez, Saavedra, and the interminable list—even to Napoleon."

—CHARLES FLETCHER LUMMIS, AUTHOR, REPORTER FOR THE
LOS ANGELES TIMES AND LAND OF SUNSHINE/OUT WEST MAGAZINES.

The movie industry landed in Southern California by chance, say film historians. The nation's first movie house, Electric Theater, opened in downtown Los Angeles in 1906. In 1907 the Los Angeles Chamber of Commerce enticed William Selig and Francis Boggs to come to the Southland to finish an outdoor scene from *The Count of Monte Cristo*. With 365 days of sunshine, the movie was soon complete, and then *The Power of the Sultan* (1908) began on its heels. The first part of *Sultan* was shot on a vacant lot at Olive and 7th Streets, next to a Chinese laundry, hardly a star-studded beginning for an industry that would shortly put Hollywood on the map of the world.

In 1909 D. W. Griffith produced many outdoors scenes on vacant lots in Los Angeles; thus the term "lot" became synonymous with "studio." In 1911 the first permanent movie studio opened in Hollywood. David and William Horsley, English brothers who owned the Centaur Company in New Jersey, flipped a coin. One side and they'd head for Florida. Heads won and a studio on Sunset Boulevard and Gower Street (where CBS is today) opened. The building had once been a tavern, then a Salvation Army hall, and then became the Nestor Studios (later to be taken over by Carl Laemmle and called Universal Pictures). The Horsley brothers' first film was *The Best Man Wins*.

Other filmmakers fled the East, and in 1912 Mack Sennett, of the Keystone Studios, produced two of his first Keystone Cops movies (often filmed at Echo Park). In 1913 Cecil B. De Mille made *Squaw Man* in partners with Jesse L. Lasky and Samuel Goldwyn. It was filmed

"That's what I object to about modern movies. Any paltry sweetheart can take their clothes off and she's interesting to the average audience."

—CHARLIE CHAPLIN, *SHOW*, JUNE 1972

in a rented barn in Hollywood on the corner of Selma and Vine. From 1912 through 1914, Mack Sennett, who was an ex-vaudevillian performer, hired a crew of stars for his blossoming film industry. When Ford Sterling, his top star, left, Sennett hired English comic Charlie Chaplin at the princely sum of $150 a week.

Chaplin premiered in *Making A Living* (1914) and made 35 more short comedies that year. His second short, *Kid Auto Races*, introduced "The Little Tramp," the Chaplin persona for which he is best known. Chaplin and Marie Dressler starred in the first full-length comedy, *Tillie's Punctured Romance*, in 1914.

In the beginning, Hollywood and its players tried hard to be straight-laced and proper. Yet, Hollywood was awash with bohemian-style living. Hollywood emerged in the American consciousness as a magical source of sexual imagery. From the early movie days through the 1920s, Hollywood served as the primer for a new sexual revolution. As actor-director Raoul Walsh said, "The Roaring Twenties did not come to Hollywood. They were born there."

145

Portrait

COMEDY'S FLUSTERED STAR
Stan Laurel

Known to millions of film buffs, comedy aficionados, and those who love old movies, Arthur Stanley Jefferson (1890-1965) was born in Ulverston, England. Leaving school at 16 to work with his father, an actor and theater manager, Stan adopted the stage name Laurel. He was a talented actor and gifted comedian who became a film legend who excelled as the straight man for Oliver Hardy.

Stan and his great friend, then unknown Charlie Chaplin, arrived in New York with Fred Karno's vaudeville theater group in a show called "Wow-Wow" that later became "A Night in an English Music Hall." In 1917 he made his first film, *Nuts in May*.

***Stan Laurel was the straight-man
half of Laurel and Hardy.***
*Courtesy of the Photo Department
Los Angeles Public Library*

"Forget Chaplin. Stan was the greatest."

—Buster Keaton, an appropriate epitaph for Stan Laurel

Stan met Oliver Hardy in 1919 while making *The Lucky Dog*. Between 1926 and 1952 they made 117 films together. In 1932 their film *The Music Boy* won an oscar for "Best Live Action Short Subject."

In 1924, Stan started working with Hal Roach as a scriptwriter and idea man. Stanley had a hand in directing, creating gags, writing, and editing virtually every film that he did with Hardy, which counted more than 70. Biographers call him a workaholic, spending 16 to 20 hours a day at the studio. After a series of personal and marital problems throughout the 1930s, Stan found his greatest enjoyment and comfort from making people laugh.

In 1934, legend has it, Stan had a falling out with producer Roach over the movie *Babes in Toyland*, a classic for the comedy duo, yet they continued working for the studio until 1940. It was that year that they signed with 20th Century Fox and made their last (and most dismal, some say) movie together, *Atoll K* (1950), a French/Italian film and a commercial and critical failure.

In 1960, Stan Laurel was given a special Oscar for Lifetime Achievement. He deeply regretted that his longtime comedy collaborator, Oliver Hardy who died in 1957, was no longer living to share the limelight.

Stan Laurel made 182 films in a career lasting 33 years. He passed away on February 23, 1965 at the age of 74.

Scandal, from secret weddings, orgies, and drug-induced suicides, seemed to be the future of Hollywood in the 1920s, and headlines throughout the country told the juicy details. When "English" actor-turned-director William Desmond Taylor was murdered on February 1, 1922, on the heels of another scandal concerning the comic Fatty Arbuckle, Southern California and America seemed to have had enough.

When the story came out, in its shocking and minute detail, it was discovered that the debonair Taylor (once thought to be the most sought-after bachelor and of the highest quality—thus preserving some standard in Hollywood) was actually William Cunningham Deane-Tanner, an Irish-born son of a British army colonel. Although all of movieland and America thought Taylor was an unmarried "catch," in actuality he had deserted his wife and child.

The details of Taylor's life and death read better than a made-for-TV movie or a detective novel and have been included in various film documentaries about the underside of Hollywood. Well before the tabloids we find in today's supermarkets, all of America gobbled up the tales of Taylor being murdered by his own brother, by a drifter, by a homosexual lover. While there is still plenty of conjecture floating around, even on the Internet, the case has never been solved.

With the scandals surrounding William Desmond Taylor and the kidnapping of evangelist Aimee Semple McPherson, along with other

CHARLIE CHAPLIN
Tramp Around Town

British-born actor and comic star Charlie Chaplin (1889-1977) arrived in the United States in 1910, and by 1914 had made his first feature film for Keystone Studios. He was a close friend of comedy great Stan Laurel.

Born Charles Spencer, he first introduced his character the "Little Tramp" in a short film called *Kid Auto Races*. Personified with a bowler hat, a funny walk, and over-sized clothing, by 1919 Chaplin was successful enough to open his own studio, United Artists, with D. W. Griffith, Douglas Fairbanks, and Mary Pickford.

In the 1940s the House Un-American Activities Committee attacked Chaplin for alleged communist sympathies and for moral turpitude. While the first was never proven, history recounts many a basis for the second during the wild-party eras of Hollywood. Angered and hurt, Chaplin moved his family to Switzerland. In 1972, with the witch hunts of the McCarthy era a nasty memory of the past, he returned to the warm embrace of Hollywood. Charlie Chaplin received a British knighthood in 1975, as he had never given up his British citizenship.

Known as "Little Tramp,"
Charlie Chaplin was introduced
in the short film Kid Auto Races.
Courtesy of the Photo Collection
Los Angeles Public Library

colorful Hollywood characters on the minds and wagging tongues of the country, it seemed that America's and Southern California's straight-laced religious figures were threatening to shut down the film industry and run the whole bohemian crew out.

Hollywood was forced to monitor itself. Thus was established the Hays Office, technically known as the Motion Picture Producers and Distributors of America Inc. William H. Hays, once Postmaster General, came from Washington to Los Angeles in 1922 and laid down the rules: No more drugs, no more wild parties, no more sexual scandals of any sort. And with Hays's approval, studios set up spying systems to keep their flock out of trouble and out of the newspaper headlines that were rampant after the death of William Desmond Taylor.

Portrait

CARY GRANT
Still a Heartthrob

Cary Grant (1904-1986) was a legendary film star and the quintessence of suave. Born in Bristol, England, he was one of thousands of underfed and scruffy boys in the less-wealthy neighborhoods. But Grant wanted more and began hanging around theaters and music halls. He joined a comedy troupe at 14, which toured the United States in 1920. After appearing in New York, he headed to California in 1931 for a screen test at Paramount. It was then that Archibald Alexander Leach became Cary Grant.

Grant's first film was *This Is the Night* (1932), but it wasn't until he played with Katharine Hepburn in *Sylvia Scarlett* (1935) that Grant found his niche. In 1937 Grant ended his contract with Paramount and went on to make scores of highly successful, slightly screwball comedies including *Holiday, Bringing Up Baby,* and *The Bachelor and the Bobbysoxer* (with Shirley Temple). In 1939 he stared with Douglas Fairbanks, Victor McLaglen, and Sam Jaffee in the classic *Gunga Din*. It was filmed in Lone Pine, California, not the northern frontiers of India as it seems in the movie. A little-known film fact is that Grant would have done anything to make that movie.

In Fairbanks's autobiography, *The Salad Days*, he says, "When I asked Cary which part he intended to play, he answered, 'Whichever one you don't want! I want us to be together in this so badly—I think the two of us, plus old McLaglen as our top sergeant, MacChesney, will make this picture more than just another big special'." Eventually it was decided that Grant would play the debonair but kooky Cutter.

How the matter was settled is a delightful footnote to movie history. Wrote Fairbanks, "We finally settled the matter by tossing a coin! That was how I became 'Sergeant Ballantine,' who wants to leave the army for Miss Fontaine, and Cary became the ebullient, funny cockney 'Sergeant Cutter.' Until his death, Cary and I always addressed each other as Cutter and Ballantine, from that film of 1939!"

In 1941, Grant was nominated for an Academy Award for Best Actor for *Penny Serenade*. In 1944 he was nominated again for *None but the Lonely Heart*, yet was overlooked once more. The Academy finally bestowed upon him an honorary award in 1969. For Grant film buffs it's difficult to decide on favorites, which include *Arsenic and Old Lace* (1944), Britisher Hitchcock's *Notorious* (1946) with Ingrid Bergman, with Ann Sheridan in *I Was a Male War Bride* (1949), Hitchcock's *North by Northwest* (1959), or *Charade* (1963) with Audrey Hepburn. Cary Grant retired from the screen in 1966.

Portrait

ART LINKLETTER
Man of Letters and Man of Ages

Nearing 90 years young, Art Linkletter has never stopped us from saying the darnedest things, just as he did for years on his popular television show, *House Party*, and for CBS radio for 25 years. He penned the award-winning book with the same name as his television show *Kids Say the Darnedest Things*, and it was one of the top 14 best-sellers in American publishing history and #1 for two consecutive years. It is one of 23 books Art Linkletter has written. His most recent national bestseller is *Old Age Is Not for Sissies*.

Today, active and vital, Linkletter still wows crowds regardless of age or occupation and is very much the role model.

Born in Moosejaw, Saskatchewan, July 1912, transplanted to Southern California as a child, and graduated from San Diego State University, Linkletter now serves as the president of the University of Southern California's Center of Aging, which is the home of one of the nation's top three geriatric hospitals. He says he especially enjoys talking to people age 40 and older because he believes that this is the age when people should look at their lives and examine their lifestyles.

The son of a Baptist minister, Linkletter practices what he preaches. He starts the day with stretches and floor exercises, swims 25 to 30 laps, lifts weights, rides a stationary bike, surfs, and skis three or four weeks each winter. His favorite pastime, say his biographers, is speaking out for the rights of seniors and debunking myths on aging. He's a champion for senior rights including those of dignity, privacy, and medical disclosure. This remarkable man's schedule consists of 75 paid speaking engagements annually, numerous board meetings, and numerous national television appearances (most recently, a weekly program with Bill Cosby).

After more than a 60-year career, what makes Linkletter continue to speak at conferences and seminars? "I enjoy it," he says. "I'm doing what I like to do more than anything else and I feel what I'm saying matters. It's a calling, not a job."

❖Portrait

MAKING A STATEMENT
Michael J. Fox

ℬiographers say that Michael J. Fox is one of Canada's most successful exports. From the start, America has been charmed by his boyish good looks, comedy talent and now his frankness about the disease that is plaguing his career and his life. Fox has Parkinson's Disease and has taken on the task to inform his fans and the public about its effects.

Born in 1961 in Edmonton, Alberta, Canada, Fox began acting at 15. He landed television roles early on and moved to Los Angeles at 18. His most remembered roles of the early days were in *Family Ties*, where he starred as the neo-conservative son obsessed with money and politics, Alex P. Keaton. Fox won three Emmy Awards for that role. His film career excelled in the *Back to the Future* series. Film buffs will remember him in *The American President, The Frighteners,* and *Mars Attacks! Spin City*, a series set in New York City, brought Fox back to America's television sets. Because of the debilitating effects of his disease (which he kept secret for years), Fox has recently decided to slow the pace, yet not let the condition divorce him from fans as he plans to continue his career.

Michael J. Fox is one of Hollywood's finest and best-liked actors.
Courtesy of the Photo Collection
Los Angeles Public Library

NOTABLE BRITISH AND CANADIAN
Film Personalities

Vivien Leigh (1913-1967)
best remembered for roles in *Gone With the Wind* and *A Streetcar Named Desire*.

Lawrence Olivier (1907-1989)
called the greatest actor ever.

Peter Sellers (1925-1980)
magnificent comic and straight actor.

● ●

Dozens of Hollywood's Glitterati
Came from the British Isles or Canada
Including These Celebrities

Pamela Sue Anderson	Paul Gross	Rick Moranis
Julie Andrews	Hugh Grant	Mike Myers
Alan Ayckbourn	Alex Guiness	David Niven
Dan Aykroyd	Phil Hartman	Maureen O'Hara
Freddie Bartholomew	Natasha Henstridge	Barry Pepper
Pierce Brosnan	Alfred Hitchcock	Mary Pickford
Richard Burton	Bob Hope	Sarah Polley
Michael Caine	Anthony Hopkins	Callum Keith Rennie
Neve Campbell	Joshua Jackson	Diana Rigg
Jim Carrey	Deborah Kerr	Devon Sawa
Hayden Christensen	Angela Landsbury	Jane Seymour
Ronald Coleman	Art Linkletter	William Shatner
Sean Connery	Ida Lupino	Martin Short
Roy Dupris	James Mason	Dame Elizabeth Taylor
Dave Foley	Malcolm McDowell	Emma Thompson
Michael J. Fox	Ray Milland	Alex Trebek
Victor Garber	Haley & John Mills	Harland Williams
John Geilgud	Roger Moore	

Portrait

TALIESIN EVANS
Journalist and Bard 1843 – 1926

*B*orn in the heart of the Welsh country, Taliesin Evans was drawn to Southern California in the 1870s and became a staff writer for the *Los Angeles Star*, *San Diego Union* (now the *Union-Tribune*) and a book reviewer and reporter for the *San Francisco Chronicle*. Often forgotten for his journalism, the Welshman who lived in California and in the British Isles is remembered for his poetry. He served as president of the Welsh Cymrodorian Society, and was considered in his time to be one of the most able poets in the Welsh tongue in America.

At age 19, he left home and worked in the mines in British Columbia for seven years. Here he gained insight into the working class struggle, which later was mirrored in work.

He was the author of *American Citizenship*, which was used for many years by those seeking citizenship. He also wrote a group of children's poems collected in *Babyland Ballads*.

A number of years before his death, Evans was given the honor of becoming the Welsh Bard, a high honor amongst the Welsh people.

*T*he British Isles and Canadian connection to arts and entertainment provide interesting connections to the Southern California we know today. For instance, Bill Evans, son of Hugh, an Englishman originally from Lincolnshire, England, was the landscape architect for Disneyland, Disney World, and EuroDisney. He was the first to sculpt Disney characters out of cypress tress and other plants.

In an interview with *Orange County Business Journal* reporter Susan Deemer (September 7, 1998), Evans said, "Walt showed me

"Bill Evans is one of the living gods, walking and breathing and carrying his knowledge on. He is an integral part of every project [at Disney's kingdoms] that has ever been done and that is being done now. He has so many pearls of wisdom. Every time you are with him, he will come up with something. I guess that's what 88 years does."

—PAUL COMSTOCK, PRINCIPAL LANDSCAPE ARCHITECT
FOR WALT DISNEY IMAGINEERING, *ORANGE COUNTY BUSINESS JOURNAL*, 1998

these pictures from Europe and said, 'How long would it take you to make these into Disney characters?'" The topiaries took decades to grow in Europe, but under Walt Disney's direction, Evans pulled it together in about two years, forming character's legs by bending branches into metal frames and chicken wire.

His father, Hugh Evans, was a businessman and real estate tycoon with subdivisions in San Diego and Riverside County, but the elder Evans' heart was in the garden. He was one of the founding members of the California Botanical Gardens, about 1000 acres of land that was established in 1927 in Brentwood's (Los Angeles) Manderville Canyon. Hugh Evans was married to Muriel E. Morgan of San Luis Rey, California, another British colonial enclave near San Diego. The former Miss Morgan was born near London, England, and educated in London and California.

Portrait

JOHN T. GAFFEY
Writer and Entrepreneur

John T. Gaffey was born in Galway, Ireland, in 1860 and came to America and then to California by way of the Isthmus of Panama, landing in San Francisco. Gaffey's mother, Ann E. Tracey Gaffey, was obviously a woman of spirit. Widowed before leaving Ireland, Mrs. Gaffey was determined to bring her children up in moral circumstances and bought a cattle and sheep ranch at Santa Cruz.

Gaffey had inherited his mother's determination and at age 19, became a reporter for the *Santa Cruz Courier* and the *Santa Cruz Herald*. After heroics during the reign of bandits led by Ignacio Lejada, a first lieutenant of the notorious Vasquez, Gaffey was appointed as a clerk for the Supreme Court of the Southern district. Subsequently he was a member of the board of Equalization for Southern California, the Los Angeles City Council, and the Los Angeles School Board. In 1894, he became the managing editor of the *Los Angeles Herald*.

When Gaffey married Arcadia Bandini, daughter of Juan and Dolores Bandini, he joined one of California's most prestigious and oldest families. In later years, the Gaffeys made their home in San Pedro.

A major developer of Southern California, the multi-talented John T. Gaffey was the early managing editor of the Los Angeles Herald.
Courtesy of the Photo Collection/Los Angeles Public Library

Literary Influences

From the very beginning, Southern California seemed to call on those from the British Isles and Canada to recount and explain the glories and the downsides of life in the state. Hugo Reid wrote about the lives of the Native Americans in what is now Pasadena and the San Gabriel Valley.

Englishman Horace Annesley Vachell, who ranched in Southern California, wrote about early ranching life in his 1899 novels, *A Drama in Sunshine* and *The Procession of Life*. Vachell, who lived in the English Colony in Riverside, is said to have been the first to introduce polo to the area (although others dispute that) by playing the game with the vaqueros on his ranch. He refused to be pulled down by the "overworked" side of Californians, yet knew the dark side of ranching.

"When I came to California a year ago," says one of Vachell's characters in *The Procession of Life (1899)*, "the faces of the men and women—ay, and the children—shocked me. The sun seemed to have sucked from them the good red blood as it sucks the sap from the grass. I traveled about between Monterey and San Diego, but leaving out the Spanish, I saw few smiles and heard little laughter."

While Vachell's own California dreams failed in the place he called Arcadia, he kept the ideas alive with his fictional characters and with the promise of "better and happier days, when life on the Pacific Slope will be purged of what is mean and sordid."

Welshman Griffith J. Griffith donated the land for Griffith Park.
Courtesy of the Photo Collection/Los Angeles Public Library

George Wharton James, an Englishman and defrocked Methodist minister (involved in a scandal perpetuated by his mentally ill wife in the 1880s and recorded in detail in the *Los Angeles Times*), wrote of California and the desert with feeling dignity and a respect for the Native Americans. His work includes *In and Out of the Old Missions of California* (1905), *The Wonders of the Colorado*

Desert (1906), *Through Ramona's Country* (1909), *Heroes of California* (1910), and *California, Romantic and Beautiful* (1914). Literary critics say that James's work is never deep, but his hard-won optimism after the disaster of losing his church, wife, and reputation, along with his unequaled love of California, shows through all his work. These same convictions won him claim as a noted lecturer, and he said, "I believe in the buoyancy, the happiness, the radiancy, the perfection of life (*Living the Radiant Life, a Personal Narrative*, Pasadena, 1916)."

While novelists like Vachell told about the hardship and the glories of the ranch life, newspapers of the times shouted that the land was open for promise and hope and could prove the mettle of any man or woman.

Historically Speaking

For generations Southern California has been engulfed with immigrant tides. Each year orange and walnut groves, bean field, and hillslopes covered with native growth give way to the subdivider. the easily accessible areas of natural beauty with the passing of the years become smaller and fewer…This perpetual change is exciting though not always satisfying. Nevertheless, Southern California still has great interest and great beauty.

—W. W. ROBINSON, *PANORAMA*

CONCLUSION

YEARS COULD EASILY BE SPENT COMPILING AND WRITING ABOUT THE BRITISH AND CANADIAN INFLUENCE ON early Southern California. Even today, that influence continues. The *Los Angeles Times* headlines of the historical and contemporary scope of that influence were made recently with an article by *Los Angeles Times* reporter Evelyn Iritani (November 7, 2000). She writes, "In 1999, British firms spent $234 billion on foreign purchases, making them the world's top exporter of cash, stock and other securities. Of that $135.8 billion was invested in the United States, the bulk of which ended up in California."

Since the contributions from immigrants continue today, I must apologize to those I have slighted or not recognized. It seems every day that a new bit of information surfaces about their efforts and assistance. In the final days of research, the histories, stories, and words of even more influential and important British, Scottish, Irish, Welsh and Canadian immigrants have come to my attention.

For instance, noted California photographer Frederic Hamer Maude, who came to California from England as a remittance man, created a photographic collection of the years of our state as did no other. And Robert B. Evans, born in Wales and a resident of Altadena, who wrote under the nom-de-plume "Trogwy," was recommended for inclusion, as were countless others.

Alas, as stated in the Introduction, consider this book as a canvas where you can envision a broad-brush stroke giving you the feelings and images of the influence of the British and Canadians, but lacking the detail of an academic encyclopedia.

The sketch for you, one that started with Sir Frances Drake, has yet to be completed; the British and Canadian influence continues. Writers, entrepreneurs, filmmakers, actors, health seekers, and people of education and religion arrive every day from the British Isles and Canada and make their homes in Southern California. You can find them still having afternoon tea, or at a London- or Dublin-style pub, lifting a Guinness and celebrating an event that has contributed to California and her British and Candian immigrants. So the influence continues.

My hope is that you will have marveled at the scope and depth of that influence, relished the photos, heard the words of our common ancestors, and learned a bit from this book. It is further my hope that you'll use the information sections that follow as a guide to help you to discover your own roots in our state.

Eva Shaw, Ph.D., Carlsbad, California • February 2001

⇒ Census Data

England	Imperial	Kern	Los Angeles	Orange	Riverside	San Bernardino	
1960	496	3185	158950	15880	6765	9064	
1950	80	578	39141	1628	963	1450	
1940	89	500	36301	1054	674	1120	
1930	123	578	39,904	1,179	762	1,347	
1920	193	644	19,454	683	578	991	
1910	106	598	11,881	489	599	993	
1900	n/a	365	1,530	116	85	118	
1890	n/a	205	3,482	272	n/a	805	
1880	n/a	120	681	n/a	n/a	233	
1870	n/a	34	248	n/a	n/a	170	

Scotland	Imperial	Kern	Los Angeles	Orange	Riverside	San Bernardino	
1960	496	3185	158950	15880	6765	9064	
1950	33	177	12020	432	245	432	
1940	25	187	10760	215	182	293	
1930	43	178	11,836	269	208	320	
1920	64	153	4,528	143	196	244	
1910	31	154	2,454	80	182	247	
1900	n/a	4	305	61	2	39	
1890	n/a	43	748	48	0	201	
1880	n/a	27	162	n/a	n/a	34	
1870	n/a	13	65	n/a	n/a	34	

Wales	Imperial	Kern	Los Angeles	Orange	Riverside	San Bernardino	
1960	496	3185	158950	15880	6765	9064	
1950	80	578	39141	1628	963	1450	
1940	4	22	1311	29	24	44	
1930	6	25	1,879	55	27	58	
1920	19	21	1,011	43	22	46	
1910	n/a	n/a	n/a	n/a	n/a	n/a	
1900	n/a	55	1,182	47	148	209	
1890	n/a	10	123	12	n/a	29	
1880	n/a	120	681	n/a	n/a	233	
1870	n/a	34	248	n/a	n/a	170	

San Diego	San Luis Obispo	Santa Barbara	Ventura	Totals	* Including:
23952	1787	5231	3528	228838	* Scotland, Wales and Northern Ireland
4216	368	1179	582	50185	* Wales
3594	276	1049	458	45115	
3,912	289	1,214	487	49795	
2,687	274	830	279	26613	
1,621	240	503	216	17246	
219	63	116	108	2720	
1,167	266	425	195	6817	
161	110	222	98	1625	* Wales
98	76	134	n/a	760	* Wales

San Diego	San Luis Obispo	Santa Barbara	Ventura	Totals	* Including:
23952	1787	5231	3528	228838	* England, Wales and Northern Ireland
1213	107	474	164	15297	
955	72	506	127	13322	
1,016	89	607	147	14713	
626	58	408	82	6502	
371	72	227	86	3904	
13	11	9	1	445	
233	82	148	96	1599	
48	51	73	42	437	
36	34	34	0	216	

San Diego	San Luis Obispo	Santa Barbara	Ventura	Totals	* Including:
23952	1787	5231	3528	228838	* England, Scotland and Northern Ireland
4216	368	1179	582	50185	* England
113	13	27	5	1592	
179	18	43	12	2302	
154	14	28	5	1363	
n/a	n/a	n/a	n/a	n/a	
242	219	99	33	2234	
28	5	14	2	223	
161	110	222	98	1625	* England
98	76	134	n/a	760	* England

Ireland	Imperial	Kern	Los Angeles	Orange	Riverside	San Bernardino	
1960	148	715	38918	3258	1263	2099	
1950	27	219	9515	306	186	360	
1940	30	225	9789	214	157	320	
1930	38	216	8042	167	145	235	
1920	119	424	7454	157	155	400	
1910	62	540	5542	135	200	469	
1900	n/a	49	209	3	87	149	
1890	n/a	258	2170	102	n/a	379	
1880	n/a	197	725	n/a	n/a	81	
1870	n/a	96	471	n/a	n/a	78	

Canada	Imperial	Kern	Los Angeles	Orange	Riverside	San Bernardino	
1960	632	3546	177600	21151	6902	10431	
1950	11	64	4502	170	92	169	
1940	148	860	46103	1432	1067	1780	
1930	n/a	n/a	n/a	n/a	n/a	n/a	
1920	n/a	n/a	n/a	n/a	n/a	n/a	
1910	201	510	11906	630	914	1386	
1900	n/a	28	316	8	22	36	
1890	n/a	142	2537	292	n/a	1255	
1880	n/a	72	420	n/a	n/a	142	
1870	n/a	31	65	n/a	n/a	32	

Totals	England	Scotland	Wales	Ireland	Canada	Total
1960	228838	*	*	**	256044	484882
1950	50185	15297	*	12160	5577	83219
1940	45115	13322	1592	12357	56831	129217
1930	49795	14713	2302	10218	n/a	77028
1920	26613	6502	1363	10456	n/a	44934
1910	17246	3904	n/a	8297	17747	47194
1900	2720	445	2234	752	486	6637
1890	6817	1599	223	4394	5940	18973
1880	1625	437	*	1680	1096	4838
1870	760	216	*	1107	372	2455

San Diego	San Luis Obispo	Santa Barbara	Ventura	Totals	
6072	455	1149	839	54916	* *Excluding:* ** *Northern Ireland*
962	68	362	155	12160	
983	94	407	138	12357	
806	89	380	100	10218	** *Northern Ireland*
968	191	474	114	10456	
667	249	291	142	8297	
29	17	115	94	752	
730	336	256	163	4394	
176	207	179	115	1680	
172	101	189	n/a	1107	

San Diego	San Luis Obispo	Santa Barbara	Ventura	Totals
25704	1683	4741	3654	256044
470	15	44	40	5577
3708	303	861	569	56831
n/a	n/a	n/a	n/a	n/a
n/a	n/a	n/a	n/a	n/a
1337	194	430	239	17747
49	7	10	10	486
966	265	278	205	5940
123	99	124	116	1096
122	56	66	n/a	372

Key:

* Including

** Excluding

APPENDIX II ⟹ Southern California Libraries, Genealogical Collections and History Centers

Bancroft Library, University of California Berkeley, Berkeley, CA 94720-6000: This library holds what some California history scholars believe to be the best collection of books on the state. The history of Hubert Howe Bancroft, why he donated the material and why he undertook to establish this invaluable resource is compelling.

Cal State Los Angeles Library, 54151 State College Dr., Los Angeles, CA 90032: 21,749 films; 280 fiche; Guide to Public Records Office of England; marriage notices for U.S. 1785-1794; National Archives Guide to Paris, France; other genealogy books interfiled with large book collection.

Cal State Northridge Library, 18111 Nordhoff St., Northridge, CA 91330: Film room has a 41-page catalog of holdings, Denmark censuses, NJ directories, Luxembourg census, old books, newspapers on microfiche, genealogy books interfiled with book collection.

Carlsbad City Library, 1250 Carlsbad Village Dr., Carlsbad, CA 92008: Kentucky Deed books; 19 volumes of official roster of Soldiers, Sailors, and Marines; Draper Manuscripts; 53,000 microfiche collection; 615 films, 16,200 genealogical books.

Claremont College Library, 800 Dartmouth St., Claremont, CA 91711: 6,543 periodicals; 28,000 microfilm; 960,000 microfiche; Nordic collection; French, German, and Danish Biographies; Biographie Universelle in French—45 volumes, books interfiled.

Daughters of the British Empire, PO Box 872, Ambler, PA 19002-0872: The Daughters of the British Empire (D.B.E) is a charitable, voluntary, non-political, non-sectarian, non-profit American society of women of British and Commonwealth birth or ancestry. Its members are professionals, business women and homemakers who share common interests and heritage, who meet regularly for business and social events with the common cause of philanthropy. The Society was founded in the United States in the year 1909 as the Imperial Order, Daughters of the Empire in the U.S.A., and became the National Society, daughters of the British Empire in the U.S.A. in 1920. The Society has a membership in the continental United States and Hawaii of approximately 5,000. It is affiliated with the Imperial Order, Daughters of the Empire in Canada (I.O.D.E.); the Victorian League, London, England; and the General Federation of Women's Clubs in the United States. The British Home in California Ltd., incorporated in 1930, is in Sierra Madre (Los Angeles), California. The Western Home is in the foothills of the of the Sierra Madre Mountains and has 6 separate cottages, dining room, kitchen and offices surrounding a central garden. Covered walkways join the buildings. There are single rooms for 37 residents.

Grant R. Brimhall Library (genealogy section), 1401 E. Janss Rd., Thousand Oaks, CA 91362, (805) 449-2660. Hours: M-Th: 10 am to 9 pm, Fri: 10 am to 6 pm, Sat: 10 am to 5 pm, Sun: 1 pm to 5 pm.

Huntington Beach Public Library, 7111 Talbert Ave., Huntington Beach, CA 92648: 700 genealogy books; 7,000 films; 36,000 fiche;

official roster of ND soldiers, sailors, and marines; Adj. General's Report state of Kansas; L.A. and Orange County obituary files.

Immigrant Library, P. O. Box 7369, Burbank, California, 91510-7369: 5,000 books, 400 films, 3,000 fiche. German subjects make up 50 percent of the collection. Germany telephone books and other distinguished German collections.

Los Angeles Public Library—History and Genealogy Department, 630 W. 5th St., Los Angeles, CA 90071, (213) 228-7400 or fax (213) 228-7409: 57,000 books; 507 periodicals; 5,254 films; 18 fiche; great collections of family, county histories, and heraldry; map collection.

National Archive Pacific Southwest Region, 24000 Avila Rd., (first floor—east entrance) Laguna Niguel, CA 92677-6719, (714) 643-4241: Complete set of all U.S. censuses from 1790 to 1920; Index to wars 1812, Rev. War, Spanish-American, Mexican; some military service records including muster rolls, pay vouchers; War pension and bounty land application files; some indexes to ports of arrival.

Pasadena Public Library, 285 East Walnut St., Pasadena, CA 91101, (818) 405-4052: 240,000-book library with 1,500 genealogical books, 100,000 films, 750 fiche, a family history collection, and a West Virginia history collection.

Pomona Public Library, 625 S. Grey Ave., Pomona, CA 91766: 5,700 genealogical books; 300 film; 2500 fiche; index to Irish wills; English convicts in Colonial America, 4 volumes; pension rolls of 1835; NJ Index of Wills; Pioneer Baptist Church Records of south central Kentucky and Tennessee.

Sherman Library and Gardens, 2647 East Coast Highway, Corona Del Mar, CA 92625, (714) 673-1880: the library contains over 20,000 books, pamphlets and other printed items. It also has thousands of maps and photographs and a considerable amount of material on microfiche including all the back issues of the *Los Angeles Times* from its inception in 1881.

Sons of Revolution Library, 600 S. Central, Glendale, CA 91204, (818) 240-1775: 25,000 genealogical books, 125 periodicals, bound Boston Transcript, 35 volumes Archives of Maryland, 121 Pennsylvania Archives, 140 volumes War of Rebellion, 15 volumes Rhode Island Vital Records, 222 Volumes MA Vital Records, Virginia collections.

Southern California Genealogical Society, 417 Irving Dr., Burbank, CA 91504-2408, (818) 843-7247: 6,500 genealogical books, 40 films, 2,000 fiche, Turner Collection, Brossman Collection, 245 volumes of Jones and Gandrud Alabama records, large periodical collection of over 2,000 volumes.

UCLA, University Research Library, 405 Hilgard Ave., West Los Angeles, CA 90024, (310) 825-1323, Map Library (310) 825-3526: 5-million book library with an Americana collection, city directories, GA State Gazette 1786, newspapers from Spain 1800-1900. There's a Map Library and a Young Research Library at UCLA. The UCLA Law Library can be used to locate ancestors and their neighbors in the "Decennial Digest" index located on the lower floor.

Whittier College Library, 7031 Founders Hills Rd., Whittier, CA 90602: Genealogies are interfiled with the 175,000 book collection, 400 films, 21,000 fiche, Society of Friends (Quaker) Depository Library, Quaker Necrology, an index of Quaker deaths, Quaker genealogies.

⇒ Southern California Historical Societies and Organizations

Alhambra Historical Society, 1550 W. Alhambra Rd., Alhambra, CA 91802

Altadena Heritage Society, P. O. Box 218, Altadena, CA 91003

Altadena Historical Society, P. O. Box 144, Altadena, CA 91003

Azusa Historical Society, City Hall Complex, 213 E. Foothill Blvd., Azusa, CA 91702

Baldwin Park Historical Society, P. O. Box 1, Baldwin Park, CA 91706

Buena Vista Historical Society, 7843 Whitaker Street, Buena Park, CA 90621

Burbank Historical Society, 1015 W. Olive Ave., Burbank, CA 91506

Coachella Valley Genealogical Society, P.O. Box 124, Indio, California 92202

Conejo Valley Genealogical Society, Inc., PO Box 1228, Thousand Oaks, CA 91358-0228

Costa Mesa Historical Society, 1870 Anaheim Avenue, PO Box 1764, Costa Mesa, CA 92628, (714) 631-5918

Covina Valley Historical Society, 125 E. College St., Covina, CA 91723

Daughters of the American Revolution (DAR)—
California Society; Daughters of the American Revolution (DAR),
Covina California Chapter, 2441 Cameron Avenue, Covina, CA 91724

Downey Historical Society, P. O. Box 554, Downey, CA 90241

Durante Historical Society, P. O. Box 263, Durante, CA 91009

Eagle Rock Valley Historical Society, 2035 Colorado Blvd., Eagle Rock, CA 90041

Echo Park Historical Society, 1471 Fairbanks Pl., Los Angeles, CA 90026

El Monte Historical Society Museum, P. O. Box 6307, El Monte, CA 91734

Federation of Orange County Historical Organizations, PO Box 4048, Santa Ana, CA 92702

Garden Grove Historical Society, 12174 Euclid Street, Garden Grove, CA 92640

Genealogical Club of Sun City, P. O. Box 175, Sun City, CA 92586

Genealogical Society of North Orange County, P. O. Box 706, Yorba Linda, CA 92686-0706

Glendale Historical Society, P. O. Box 4173, Glendale, CA 91202

Glendora Historical Society and Museum, 314 N. Glendora Ave., Glendora, CA 91740

Glendora Genealogy Group, P.O. Box 1141, Glendora, California 91740

German Genealogical Society of America, 2125 Wright Ave. C-9, La Verne, California 91750

Hemet-San Jacinto Genealogical Society, P.O. Box 2516, Hemet, California 92343

Historical Society of Southern California, 200 E. Avenue, Los Angeles, CA 90031

Historical Society of Long Beach, 781 S. Orange Ave., Monterey Park, CA 91754

Historical Society of Pomona Valley, 1569 N. Park Ave., Pomona, CA 91768

Historical Society of Southern California, 200 E. Avenue 43, Los Angeles, CA 90031

Irvine Historical Society & Museum, 18881 Van Karman Ave., Suite 1250, Irvine, CA 92612

Jewish Genealogical Society of Los Angeles, P.O. Box 55443, Sherman Oaks, CA 91413-0443, (818) 771-5554;
Jewish Genealogical Society of Orange County, 11751 Cherry Street, Los Alamitos, CA 90720;
Jewish Genealogy Society of South Orange County, 2370-1 D Via Mariposa W., Laguna Hills, CA 92643, (714) 855-4692

La Puente Valley Historical Society, P. O. Box 522, La Puente, CA 91744

Leisure World Genealogical Workshop, 2300 Beverly Manor Rd., Seal Beach, California 90740

Lomita Historical Society, 24016 Benhill Ave., Lomita, CA 90717

Los Angeles Westside Genealogical Society, PO Box 10447, Marina del Rey, CA 90295-6447

Morongo Basin Genealogical Society, P.O. Box 234, Yucca Valley, California 92284

Norwegian Genealogy Group, c/o Sons of Norway Lodge, 2006 East Vista Wy., Vista, CA 90284-3321

Palm Springs Genealogical Society, P.O. Box 2093, Palm Springs, California 92263

Pasadena Genealogical Society, P. O. Box 94774, Pasadena, CA 921109

Pasadena Historical Society, 470 W. Walnut St., Pasadena, CA 91103

Pomona Valley Genealogical Society, P.O. Box 286, Pomona, California 91768-0286, (909) 599-2166

Questing Heirs Genealogical Society, PO Box 15102, Long Beach, CA 90815-0102, (310) 596-8736

Riverside Genealogical Society, PO Box 2557, Riverside, CA 92516

San Fernando Valley Genealogical Society, 2042 Socrates Avenue, Simi, CA 90365

San Marino Historical Society, P. O. Box 80222, San Marino, CA 91118

Santa Monica Historical Society and Museum, 1345 3rd St. Promenade, Santa Monica, CA 90408

TRW Genealogical Society, One Space Park S-1435, Redondo Beach, California 90278

Universal Genealogical Society of Bellflower, 8251 Cedar Street, Bellflower, CA 90706

Vanderberg Genealogical Society, P.O. Box 814, Lompoc, California 93438

Ventura County Genealogical Society, P.O. Box 24608, Ventura, California 93002

Yorba Linda Genealogical Society, 4751 Libra place, Yorba Linda, CA 92686

BIBLIOGRAPHY

Ainsworth, Ed. "The Story of Citrus in Its Western Pilgrimage." www.sunkist.com.

Bancroft, Hubert Howe. *The Works of Humbert Howe Bancroft, History of California*, Vol. V., 1846-1848. San Francisco: The History Company Publishers, 1886.

Bowen, Edith Blumer. *Annals of Early Sierra Madre*. Sierra Madre, California: Sierra Madre Historical Society, 1950.

Block, Eugene B. *Above the Civil War, The Story of Thaddeus Lowe*. Berkeley, California: Howell-North Books, 1966.

Brooks, Joan. *Desert Padre: The Life and Writings of Father John J. Crowley*. Desert Hot Springs, CA: Mesquite Press, 1998.

Chapman, Charles C., Donald H. Pflueger, ed., Charles C. Chapman. *The Career of a Creative California*, 1853-1944. Los Angeles: Anderson, Richie & Simon, 1976.

Cleland, Robert Glass. *The Irvine Ranch of Orange County: 1810-1950*. San Marino, California: The Huntington Library, 1952.

Collings, Ruth. "Joseph Snook: English Mariner, California Don," *Journal of San Diego History*, Fall 1997, Vol. 43, Number 4.

Dakin, Susanna Bryant. *A Scotch Paisano: Hugo Reid's Life in California, 1832-1852*. Berkeley, California: University of California Press, 1939

Davies, David, ed. Letter from James Clark to Mrs. James Clark, March 17, 1856, in "An Emigrant of the Fifties," from *Quarterly Publications of the Historical Society of Southern California*, 19: 118-119, September-December 1937.

David, Margaret. "How the Hero Who Brought Water to L.A. Abruptly Fell From Grace," *Los Angeles Times*, July 25, 1993, p. M3.

Davis, William Heath. *Seventy-five Years in California*. San Francisco: J. Howell, 1929.

Deemer, Susan. "Imagine That: Some 'Imagineers' who Designed Disneyland Are Still at Work," *Orange County Business Journal*, September 7, 1998, www.ocjb.com/archives/frontstory0907.htm

Dowling, Patrick J. *Irish Californians: Historic, Benevolent, Romantic*. San Francisco: Scotwall Associates, 1998.

Dumke, Glenn S. *The Boom of the Eighties in Southern California*. San Marino, California: Huntington Library, 1966.

Eldredge, Zeoth Sinner. *California History*, Vol. 5. New York: The Century History Co., 1914.

Epstein, Daniel Mark. *Sister Aimee: The Life of Aimee Semple McPherson*. New York: Harcourt Brace Jovanovich, 1993.

Evans, Taliesan, *Overland Monthly Magazine*, March 1874, No. 3, and May 1893, No. 125.

Fogelson, Robert M. *The Fragmented Metropolis: Los Angeles, 1850-1930*. Berkeley, California: University of California Press, 1993.

Foley, Tricia. *Having Tea: Recipes & Table Settings*. New York: Clarkson N. Potter, 1987.

Forbes, Alexander. *California: A History of Upper and Lower California*. London: Smith, Elder & Co., 1839.

Ford, John Anson. *Thirty Explosive Years in Los Angeles County*. San Marino, California: The Huntington Library, 1961.

Friedricks, William B. *Henry E. Huntington and the Creation of Southern California*. Columbus, Ohio: Ohio State University Press, 1992.

Heizer, Robert F. *Elizabethan California*. Ramona, California: Ballena Press, 1974.

Hunt, Rockwell D. A.M., Ph.D. *California and Californians*, Chicago, Illinois: Lewis Publishing, 1903.

Iritani, Evelyn. "Britian Takes the Crown for Foreign Investing in California," *Los Angeles Times*, November 7, 2000.

Ives, Sarah Noble. *Altadena*. Pasadena, California: Press of the Star-News Publishing Co., 1938.

Jackson, Sheldon G. *A British Ranchero in Old California: The Life and Times of Henry Dalton and the Rancho Azusa*. Glendale, California: The Arthur H. Clark, Co., 1987.

James, George Wharton. *Heroes of California: The story of the founders of the golden state as narrated by themselves or gleaned from other sources*. Boston: Little, Brown and Co., 1910.

Kallan, Carla. "George Chaffee: A Man of Many Firsts," *Fedco Reporter*, June 1997, p. 31.

Kirkpatrick, Sidney D. *A Cast of Killers*. New York: E. P. Dutton, 1986.

Leslie, Margaret. *Rivers in the Desert: William Mulholland and the Inventing of Los Angeles*. New York: HarperCollins, 1993.

Markham, Edwin. *California the Wonderful*. New York: Heart's International Library Company, 1914.

Moulton, Candy. *The Writer's Guide to Everyday Life in the Wild West*. Cincinnati, Ohio: Writers Digest Books, 1999.

MovieThing.com. "Michael J. Fox," www.moviething.com/bios/michaeljfox

Nava, Julian and Bob Barger. *California, Five Centuries of Cultural Contrast*. Beverly Hills, California: Glencoe Press, 1976.

Newmark, Maurice H. and Marco R. *Sixty Years in Southern California, 1853-1913, Containing the Reminiscences of Harris Newmark*. Boston: Houghton Mifflin, Riverside Press Cambridge, 1930.

Papio, Debbie. "*Gunga Din*: a movie review," www.reelclassics.com/Articles/Films/gungadin-article.htm, 1997.

Patterson, Tom. *Colony for California*. Riverside, CA: Museum Press of the Riverside Museum Associates, 1996.

Pitt, Leonard and Date Pitt. *Los Angeles A to Z: An Encyclopedia of the City and County*." Berkeley, California: University of California Press, 1997.

"The Plate of Brass Reexamined: A Report Issued by the Bancroft Library," University of California, Berkeley, 1977.

Raber, Thomas R. *Wayne Gretzky, Hockey Great*. Minneapolis, Minnesota: Lerner Publishing Group, 1999.

BIBLIOGRAPHY ⇒ continued

Richardson, H. Archie. "California Tennis Dates Back to 1870s," *The Christian Science Monitor*, April 28, 1948.

Rush, Philip S. *A History of the Californias*, 2nd edition. Self-published by the author: San Diego, California, 1964.

Sinclair, Upton. *Oil*. New York: Grosset & Dunlap, 1926.

Simpich, Frederick. "Southern California at Work," *National Geographic Magazine*, November 1934, P544.

Simpson, Sir George. *Narrative of a Journey Round the World, During the Years 1841 and 1842* (2 volumes). London: H. Colburn, 1847

Starr, Kevin. *Inventing the Dream: California Through the Progressive Era*. New York: Oxford University Press, 1985.

Starr, Kevin. *Americans and the California Dream*. 1850-1915. New York: Oxford University Press, 1973.

Sterling, Christine. Southern California Historical Society, www.socalhistory.org, and from a forthcoming book, *History of El Pueblo de Los Angeles Historical Monument, Its People, Buildings and Site*, by Jean Bruce Poole.

Stevens, Errol Wayne. "Frederic Hamer Maude: A Photographer and His Collection," *Southern California Quarterly*, Historical Society of Southern California, Spring 2000, Vol. 82, No. 1.

Thorpe, James. *Henry Edwards Huntington: A Brief Biography*. San Marino, California: Huntington Library, 1996.

Tompkins, Walker A. *Santa Barbara History Makers*. Goleta, California: Kimberly Press, Inc., 1983.

Tompkins, Walker A. *Santa Barbara's Royal Rancho*. Berkeley, California: Howell-North, 1960.

Wodehouse, P.G. *The Clicking of Cuthbert*. London: H. Jenkins, 1922.

Woods, Lawrence W. *British Gentlemen in the Wild West*. New York: The Free Press, 1989.

Workman, Boyle and Caroline Walker. *Boyle Workman's The City that Grew*. Los Angeles: Southland Publishing Co., 1936.

Yoemans, Patricia Henry. *Southern California Tennis Champion Centennial*. Los Angeles: Southern California Committee for the Olympic Games, 1987.

Biography

Eva Shaw, Ph.D., is a full-time author of more than 60 award-winning books, e-books and countless magazine articles. Her recent books include Shovel It: Nature's Health Plan and Writing the Nonfiction Book. Dr. Shaw teaches writing to students worldwide through college programs connected by the Internet and Education To Go, provides workshops at writing conferences and provides courses for the University of California's extension program.

"Recently, the connection of the British Empire's contribution to Southern California came alive when my husband, Joe, and I stood together on a rainy, blustery morning in Inverness, Scotland, next to the city's World War I memorial," says Dr. Shaw. "We'd come to hike the Highlands and to 'meet' Joe's long-lost relative. Now we have Joe's picture next to the marker that is a tribute to that brave Scottish soldier, Joseph Shaw."

Dr. Shaw admits to being an avid collector of "tidbits of information, so necessary for any historian" and to being a long-time and devoted student of Southern California history.

Photo Courtesy of CeCe Canton

INDEX

TO ORDER THIS BOOK
PLEASE CALL OR WRITE:

DICKENS PRESS
P.O. BOX 4289
IRVINE, CA 92612
(800) 230-8158

Individuals: To order, please indicate the number of copies desired, and enclose check, money order, or Visa or Mastercard number and expiration date for the full amount plus $3.95 for postage for one book, $1.50 for each additional.

Quantity discounts are available to groups, organizations and companies.

VISA & MASTERCARD are accepted.

All titles are distributed in the U.S. by Dickens Press.